A NEW CREATION

A NEW CREATION

Towards a Theology of the Christian Life

by

AUGUST BRUNNER

LONDON

BURNS & OATES

This translation from the original German,
Eine neue Schöpfung: ein Beitrag zur Theologie
des christlichen Lebens (*Ferdinand Schöningh,
Paderborn*), *was made by*

RUTH MARY BETHELL

NIHIL OBSTAT: HVBERTVS RICHARDS, S.T.L., L.S.S.
CENSOR DEPVTATVS
IMPRIMATVR: E. MORROGH BERNARD
VICARIVS GENERALIS
WESTMONASTERII: DIE XIV JVNII MCMLV

MADE AND PRINTED IN GREAT BRITAIN BY
HAZELL WATSON AND VINEY LTD AYLESBURY AND LONDON FOR
BURNS OATES AND WASHBOURNE LTD
28, ASHLEY PLACE, LONDON, S.W.1

First published 1955

Table of Contents

Preface

THE question is, whether religious poverty, chastity and obedience are really means to perfection, and whether they bring man to fulfilment as man; for they seem more conducive to loss of personality. No answer is possible until we have a clear idea of the meaning of property, marriage and freedom, and *their* function in attaining to true manhood. And this presupposes clarity as to the nature of Christian perfection. That is the theme of the four chapters of this book.

As God the holy Trinity is love, self-fulfilment too can only be achieved through love. It is the way a man comes to terms with God and with his own nature made holy in baptism. But the true nature of God became humanly comprehensible to us through Jesus Christ, God become Man, and communion with God can only be attained by fellowship with Christ. To be a Christian means to be a disciple of Christ's. To the growth of selfless love and the ripening of true Christian manhood, the great realities of life should all contribute: the possession of earthly goods, the relations of the sexes, the distribution of authority in human society. But man under original sin mistakes his self-seeking self for his real self. And that is why the way to Christian perfection involves an apparent loss of self, and a blessed abundance of spiritual riches appears as an appalling void. Only through the Cross can man attain to the Resurrection.

The purpose of this book is to work these ideas out in detail and, on the basis of revelation, to show the reader how interdependent they are.

AUGUST BRUNNER

Munich, *July* 1952.

CHAPTER ONE

The Meaning of Christian Life

CHRISTIAN VOCATION

THE meaning of Christian life is given in the formula for baptism: 'I baptize thee in the name of the Father, and of the Son, and of the Holy Ghost'. The intention is clear if we remember that in the Greek it is not 'in the name' but 'into the name', 'on to the name'. A movement is indicated, a movement 'name'-wards. And name meant in those days the individual under the law, the person as such. 'In the name of the king' still means: as representing the king, the man who as king has authority and acts on his own decision as the accepted source of authority.

Baptism sets up a movement towards the three divine Persons in the one true God. Such a movement necessarily implies a relationship and admission into the intimacy of the Blessed Trinity. And as God himself is concerned, such a relationship implies dedication and sanctification. The hidden heart of God's own life is thrown open for the baptismal candidate to enter—for ever, as it is intended, for divine life is eternal. Man was cut off from so much by his first sin, and here it is all within reach again. The baptismal ceremony of bathing or washing shows how his first sin is wiped out and in its actual effects abolished. Man is cleansed to his inmost soul of every stain and every trace of guilt.

It is the same mystery that is expressed in the words: to be baptized is to be God's child. For the child belongs by nature to his parents' sphere of life, and his life depends on their life and on its whole atmosphere. Each family is a living unit, and has its own set of ideas, its own point of view, its own way of behaving, and all this is recognizable in the children. And the relationship between the three divine Persons composes a way of life that is all pure eternal love and mutual devotion —a way of life that is inaccessible to any creature as such, for it *is* God. Only by means of unmerited grace can a creature be admitted to this mysterious light. By nature, man is infinitely below it (1 Tim. 6. 16). As he is by nature, he could not endure to approach for fear of being consumed in the ineffable majesty of divine transcendence. 'No man can see me and live', said God to Moses, when he asked to be allowed to see Him face to face (Ex. 33. 20). Only when inwardly transformed, and by the action of sanctifying grace, can a man enter into the splendour of God and live from it. The heathen were well aware that God is unapproachable. But the fact was given a natural explanation. It was often held that man with his material body belonged to an opposite type of being to the gods. That is why cleansing from purely physical dirt or from pollution through illness or unclean physical processes, played such a large part in all religions. But in fact God is inaccessible to man chiefly because of man's condition through original sin. Holy Scripture intimates as much, showing us the first parents living in trustful communion with God before they sinned: walking with him as children with their father; but after their sin they were seized with fear of him, and this fear remained ever since, till Christianity restored man's 'access' to God (Rom. 5; Eph. 2. 17 f.; 3. 12).

But how is it possible for man to live in fear of his Creator? God cannot be a danger threatening a creature he himself maintains in existence, a creature that without his sustaining power would sink into nothingness. There can be no natural opposition here, there must be something individual to man that is opposed to God, an attitude of hostility that requires 'reconciliation' (Rom. 5. 10 ff.; 2 Cor. 5. 18 ff.; Col. 1. 20 ff.) before man can go to God freely.

It is all due to the fact that after the Fall man lost his intimate personal relation to God. Since he voluntarily turned away from the source of his life, he lost his immediate awareness of dependence on God's loving creative power. And thereby he lost confidence in his own being as such. His spiritual powers are weakened at the roots and can no longer so completely animate his body that it will be spiritually alive. The centre of gravity has shifted from the spirit to the feelings, if not into physical life outright. But such a life is mortal *per se*, and in man it became mortal again when the spirit lost its animating, life-giving power through the break with God. It is on that account that a man's speculations and aspirations are concerned first and foremost with keeping this life going and making it somehow safe. Before the Fall, man had first-hand experience of his own spirituality issuing from God as creative act, and mundane concerns remained utterly subordinate to the real meaning of existence. Secure in God's love and the knowledge of his own indestructibility, man was at peace. But this experience was almost totally lost and man took on a task beyond his powers, possessed of the notion that he has to maintain his existence himself. It is a good thing to endeavour to be oneself, but the means he uses are the wrong ones. By nature, man is self-seeking. His whole range of thought and activity revolves about himself as the middle point of the world. And he dare not relax his concern for a single instant for fear his existence fall to pieces. That is why he pursues his end so relentlessly, covetous for gains that are only for his own benefit. Anyone who stands in his way is a hated enemy. Nothing is permitted to the other man but what feeds his own greed, and then only to the degree that it feeds it. But the other fellow with his claims to be the centre of the universe, only admitting right of existence to what he can use for his own ends, is the object of special hatred and envy. Till the two discover common interests and to that extent find a *modus vivendi*.

Now, if God is a personal God he must be acknowledged unconditionally, and there is no other way of approaching him. To acknowledge God as God is to recognize that his being-himself is absolute, independent of everything outside himself, including me, of course; and it is to admit my own unconditional dependence on him. But that means my human ego can no longer be the centre of my existence and must unreservedly give way to divine freedom and the divine will. It means completely and unreservedly giving up my own self-centredness. Of his own accord man is no longer capable of such an attitude. It is only possible when he has a direct sense of being safe and secure in his existence, and when he has the power of spirituality which alone can bring him into union with God. It is a sort of vicious circle that he is caught in: to resume contact with God, man has to conquer his egoism; and he can do it only when he has the strength that pours into him when this contact has come about. Anyhow, he is no longer in a position to free himself from his troubles and to attain to God, even though as creature he belongs and always has belonged to him.

Only thus can we explain this monstrous thing: that man feels God to be a threat to his existence, a threat to himself, and is therefore in the very depths of his being, from his very birth, filled with antipathy and hatred towards him. For the unreserved surrender of himself to God, unaccompanied by the experience of God's generous creative love for him, must strike him as sheer self-abandonment and a plunge into the void.

Who is going to look after him, if for the sake of this remote, unknown God he ceases to do it for himself? That precious self that requires such forethought and such a concentration of energies to keep it going at all will surely collapse the moment it ceases to be the focus of all thought and action; what will happen to it when it can no longer count on every ounce of energy to defend it? It is indeed true that man's false self is threatened by God. And that this self is false is proved by the fact that man can win through to himself only by loss of self; that is, by relinquishing his supposed self.

It is not possible for man with his heritage of sin to acknowledge God wholly as God, as is called for in the mutual relationship of creature and Creator. He has a negative attitude from birth, for the broken relationship with God and the consequent reduction in his spiritual powers are inborn in him. Thus original sin is somehow double-shot, inviting to excesses in both directions at once. As sin, it cannot be a purely natural phenomenon: for the true Christian God is a personal God, and the opposite of God is therefore personal too. Yet it has some of the characteristics of natural phenomena, in that it is there without the personal responsibility of the individual, existing in him simply because he was born man. It is a fault, a loss of power— power destined to spiritualize the body and therefore effective in the natural sphere, though not issuing from it nor at home in it. And it is this natural side of original sin which tends to occupy the forefront of our minds. Hence the tendency, which is a temptation, to see in it the authentic form of original sin. On the other hand, in the religion of a personal God, moral evil is also, religiously, anti-God; and the perception that it presupposes the existence of freedom opens the way to the danger of pelagianism, which treats original sin as practically non-existent, redemption from it requiring no inward transformation of man's self.

To be dedicated to God in baptism is to put an end to God's remoteness and man's antagonism and incapacity to recognize him as God. The 'enmity' between God and man is set aside by God's action through a supernatural renewal of man; and man is reconciled to God, so that he no longer takes him for his antagonist. God does not need to be reconciled and appeased, for his love can never diminish, not even when man sins. Without love God were no longer God. Thus it is that the reconciliation of sinful man can only issue from God. But it is achieved by a new means, by baptism. In the depths of the soul the right relationship with God is re-established, and there alone. This redeeming act forms the core of that all-embracing response to God which man will wrest from himself stage by stage till he is truly redeemed, having played his part in his own redemption, as befits his dignity as a person.

But even when he is baptized, man's natural feeling still tends to the notion that to admit his dependence is to plunge into a fathomless void and lose himself. Only through faith in God's word and God's love, and strengthened by his grace, can a man take upon himself the supernatural task of being a Christian, and make room in himself for the new life which is the reverse side of apparent death. Baptism endows a man with a state of grace and a new life within him. He is no longer merely creature, he is a child of God; thus he has a relationship not only with God but with each of the three divine Persons distinctly. He is child of the Father and therefore Christ's brother and dedicated temple of the Holy Ghost. These relationships are inseparable, they belong together, just as the three Persons are but one God. They are one single dedication, *one* sanctification, *one* accepted task and *one* reward to come. But they are different from one another, corresponding to the differences between the three Persons—one relationship and three, together. The Christian is not Christ's son, nor is he the child of the Holy Spirit. And a man's attitude to each Person is distinct, while at the same time the right attitude to one divine Person inevitably brings about the right attitude to the other two Persons.

In baptism, Christian life is bestowed and assigned—and so is everything else that concerns the person as such. The inmost soul is set free and restored, so that new opportunities open up which extend beyond what man is capable of by nature, and yet are his *own* opportunities. There can be no higher aim than the one freely given him and set before him at baptism. And whatever degree of holiness a Christian may reach by the grace of God, he never goes beyond the special assignment which his baptismal dedication conferred on him, to accompany him through life. All Christianity, all Christian effort, is but so much work put in to achieve it, it is but the way leading to the goal. And the other sacraments are only there to help men to advance along the way of perfect dedication to God, either under the conditions laid down for all Christians in common, or with special charges among the company of those going the same way (priesthood, marriage).

The first step in this mysterious vocation is taken by God: he calls. He alone. He bestows the grace that no one can merit, for no creaturely act has any sort of proportion in relation to this vocation. And the next steps are impossible without God, too. But the man whom God has called and sanctified must now do his share. For the call is not to one particular human field, not to a particular side of man, but to himself as a free, self-disposing person. It is man himself that is meant, the whole man. But a whole man is one who possesses freedom and the power of choice. The unfree, purely natural sphere in man is always in God's power, as animals and plants are, and the constellations that follow the courses their God-given nature prescribes for them. But a creature that is free has the capacity to give himself freely or to refuse, and only such an one can come to have the capacity to enter into relationship with the divine Persons as such. For other forms of being, this is not even possible by grace.

CHRISTIANITY AS DISCIPLESHIP

Relations to persons are necessarily personal. And nowhere is this more evident than in dedication to the divine Persons. A relationship freely undertaken and freely maintained. But personal relations imply a sharing in the spiritual life of a person. They are non-physical, but are on that account no less real and existent. They involve a community of thought, will and feeling at the deepest level. They culminate in love, in which two people accept the same standpoint as from one common hearth—two, and yet a single source of inspiration. Henceforth, to be dedicated to God, to belong to God, can only mean: to love God, to settle in his heart and from this new hearth to live, think and act. To be baptized is to be called to the perfect love of God and to be made capable of accepting it. And Christian life is the increasing realization of this love. Love not in the form of feeling, but as a deeply lived attitude of surrender to God, of acceptance and of union with him; springing from the deepest depth of being.

Is such an attitude conceivably possible? For the pagan there was no great difficulty about imitating his gods, for those gods of his were planned on a human scale and were therefore accessible to human understanding. But even he stopped short, in all humility, of such presumption as this. When Christianity came and rejected all diminution of God's exalted majesty, it revealed the glory of the eternal God whose 'dwelling is in unapproachable light' (1 Tim. 6. 16). How should man dare to bridge the infinite distance between him and God and establish himself in his heart in order to live out of this new centre of being? How is he to know how God thinks and judges and what view he takes of things and circumstances? How should he share in this personal life which totally eludes his intelligence? Illusions and his own desires he will more likely mistake for thoughts of God, and with a candid intention to belong to God will be all too liable to fall a victim to his own imaginations.

This is a real difficulty. Man alone cannot solve it. But God has done it for him. God became man in Christ and led a truly human life on earth. Christ has made God humanly comprehensible. For his human thoughts, desires, attitudes and acts were at the same time divine, the thoughts, desires, attitudes and acts of God. In so far as they are human, we can understand them. We can establish ourselves in a human heart in love. We can take over a human attitude of mind, and act accordingly. Thus the duty of loving God turns into an obligation to love Christ, and with him and in him the Father through the Holy Spirit. Dedication to the Holy Trinity is also, through the incarnation, union with Christ. Through baptism a Christian is a part of the mystical body of Christ. To dedicate oneself to God means henceforth 'to be of the same mind which Christ Jesus shewed' (Phil. 2. 5); it means more and more to 'invoke always the name of the Lord Jesus Christ' (Col. 3. 17); that is to say, to do as Christ would do here and now, and to do it according to his mind. Thus to be a Christian means to strive no longer to live to oneself, centred upon oneself, but centred upon the heart of Jesus (Gal. 2. 20). Through trustful loving intercourse, day by day, the Christian will come to understand Christ better and better and, basing his life on this understanding, will live and act more and more freely and spontaneously in accordance with it. Thus he will gradually make the redemption come true in every part of his own life and of his environment. The redemption is not like the blind indeterminate working of a physical force, simply breaking out in all directions at once, but it is the act of the eternal Christ being carried on to completion through the whole course of human history. Christians provide the setting for this progressive redemption and are its instruments, in all freedom and love. The Church is Christ's life prolonged, it is Christ living on. There is only one redemption because there is only one adoption, which is Son-ship through Christ. We can be children of the Father only by sharing in Christ's Son-ship. And only because the relationship is a purely personal one, and not, as among men, at the same time and above all a natural one, is such sharing possible at all.

Therefore Christ is the only door by which to enter into divine life (John 10. 9); he alone enables us to love God. Without him, without his grace, this love would be an illusion.

Christianity is thus, essentially, discipleship, fellowship for life with God made Man, with Jesus Christ, in acknowledgement of his absolute and unsurpassable dignity as God's Son. He is authority in person. Discipleship means that the disciple accepts the utterances and opinions of the master as being right and good from the very fact that they come from him; he first puts them to the proof and then he advises his disciples to do likewise. Moreover, in this personal relationship the disciple discovers that he has access to a means of extending the scope of ordinary life which would otherwise be closed to him, for his own experience and his own efforts could never reach so far.

And this discipleship has nothing accidental about it: it is, rather, deeply grounded in the nature of Christian revelation. New forms of reality must indeed at some point be worked out experimentally, there is no other way by which they could become known. Not any amount of explanation and comparison can make a man born blind understand what colour is, as distinct from the other qualities things possess. But a quality is a metaphysical reality. And realities pertaining to persons can only be perceived in persons. This is particularly true in regard to strictly personal realities, as opposed to the sub-personal levels of human existence: the personal ones are more strongly individualized, and thus to a much greater degree unique and distinct. On the physical plane, on the other hand, creatures of the same kind are so alike that to know one is, practically speaking, to know them all; this is the basis of the natural sciences and their system of laws. But as soon as we have to do with life, within the one species individual differences are apparent that conform to no law and have a validity of their own. And most of all in the spiritual sphere, as we have seen. So that a general view of the species is here insufficient, because it leaves out of account the element of uniqueness, which is here the important one.

Now where there is personality, there must be a group to endorse the fact: to observe and put on record the existence of that self-possession and self-awareness that characterize personality as such. Only in so far as a person's acts are accompanied by our understanding of them and we place ourselves in the same position in order to adopt the same viewpoint, gaining his view of the world—which is a world in itself: only thus can we do him justice. But this penetration into a personality is only possible when the person concerned allows it. Otherwise it is a denial of that basic self-possession of his. Things can be probed into by all and sundry, and remain indifferent. But as soon as we deal with persons, a basis of acknowledgement by a group has to be assumed. These conditions are *sine qua non* when the personality in question is of a very high order. We can lay down the principle that the first independent apprehension of a given reality is the act of a very small number of people, and the higher it stands in the scale of being the fewer they will be. All other people's access is only second-hand and by after-effect. This is the source of faith.

But if the personality concerned is of a higher order, not only in the possession of certain external qualities, but essentially, the group-relationship formed will be that of master and disciples. In the master's perfect life, the disciple discovers facts that are unique and are to be experienced nowhere but in his company. Such initial experience is spontaneous and inarticulate. Subsequently, if no act of repulsion intervenes, the life, attitude and acts of the master will become the disciple's model of behaviour, the master himself being there as guarantor of their truth and rightness.

Discipleship is a relationship between two persons—a movement surges up from his own inmost being and the disciple is admitted into his master's being. In the process he undergoes transformation, at the same time contributing to his own transformation. There are no new impositions: the master is no stranger to his disciple when his inmost soul unites with his. But there is an apparent contradiction: one man is exerting influence on another, extremely profound and decisive influence, and yet the freedom of the man thus influenced is not only safeguarded, it has actually entered upon a stage of great expansion. If the encounter with the master had never taken place, the disciple would never have become what he now is. But the encounter is pure reality, and as such it is gift and grace in the strictest sense. Where true discipleship exists, the influence of the master is accepted in perfect freedom, with the immediate effect of increasing the whole scope of freedom. For in the master the disciple discerns many possibilities of his own of which he was formerly unaware, and he sees at last how he can best come to himself, and he thus grows stronger in every respect. The movement that carries him to the master, issuing as it does from his own inmost being, is more purely his own act than his usual actions are, springing from less intrinsic motions. The disciple has established contact with something quite new, which is dependent on him, and on the other disciples, first for its *raison d'être*, then for its propagation. Nonetheless, being a disciple remains a free act on the part of the disciple; it is a grace and it is independent action both at once, and on the level of personality the two are not mutually exclusive at all. It is, in fact, a basic principle of personality that it only comes to itself and to awareness of its own possibilities in relation to another person. Only God, *ens a se*, moves purely and absolutely of his own volition alone, and here, too, only in personal communion within the Trinity.

Thus discipleship is a source of new knowing and of a new way of life, and is so of its very nature. From the master's own person comes the first authentic impulse. Words and acts are so many forms by which his life is revealed. He is loved and revered, and his example works as it were spontaneously, completely transforming the disciple, from his inmost soul radiating outward. The disciple is changed in his more external characteristics too, right down to the way he conducts himself in public. He becomes like his master in behaviour. It all occurs without any giving of orders, laying down of laws or issuing of commands, all from the one free spiritual impulse. Prescriptions and ordinances are the appurtenances of second-hand relationships, but discipleship is first-hand and makes the rest to some extent super-erogatory. It is on this level of discipleship, and here alone, that St. Augustine's word has full force: *Ama et fac quod vis*: You shall love, and then you may do what you like.

Growing more and more like their master, the disciples form a group together, apart from the rest. They understand one another without having to say much. Certain words take on a new meaning. Certain things can be taken for granted, leaving other people puzzled. *One* spirit animates them, the spirit of the master, and holds them together as individuals and fellows. Even when they are apart, their acts and words are of the same stamp. They reveal the deep imprint of the master on their minds. And inasmuch as they reflect the master himself in their life and ways, they win disciples for him even among those who never saw him, and thus spread his influence over great distances in space and time. Thus spirit and personality are shown to be more powerful than barriers of space and time, however much they remain, when human and bound to the body, subject to their condition.

Discipleship is of its very nature a personal relationship, and it arises when a man appears on the scene with imposing and exalted qualities which arouse in others the desire to imitate and follow him, because of what he is and what his way of life reveals. Knowledge thus impar-ted is not academic or abstract: it is alive and founded once for all on trust. This is, incidentally, the essential basis of all forms of knowledge. Compared with this living relationship, the written word is second-hand; which explains the fact that the greatest masters did not write themselves: they had more effective means at their disposal. And whenever master and disciple come together, not abstract learning, but wisdom, the mystery of existence and of man, are the dominant concerns. Personal excellence of some kind may give rise to other forms of relationship—that of teacher and pupils, leader and followers, lord and servant or subject. But all are based on discipleship, for all man's knowing and doing imply the existence of personality and freedom.

It is no accident that discipleship is at its best in the religious sphere. All the great founders of religions are men who gathered disciples around them. Founders of religions are always men who try to introduce a higher form to replace the existing one, the new form in its experimental stage throwing light on the old form and showing up its deficiencies. And the higher form of a religion is always one that makes more room for the personal aspect of divinity. Where men worship almost depersonalized worldly powers, there is no need for a founder and master, it is a sort of religion that arises of its own account and thrives on current events and the deliberate pressure brought to bear on individuals and groups. Here, no one form of experience is better than another: some are more potent, some are less. That is all.

But discipleship has a true greatness of its own. Essentially it is one of the finest kinds of relationship that exist. But when the master is only mortal man, the ultimate depths of personality remain unplumbed. These depths are reserved for God the Creator, and when a man attempts to force his way into this sanctuary, leadership degenerates into seduction. In himself, no man is faultless and wholly good. And therefore the purely human relationship of master and disciple has limitations the transgression of which brings its own retribution. The master is liable to pride and the abuse of power, and the disciple forfeits his independence and freedom and becomes involved in damaging entanglements.

It is clearly in the nature of things that in the religion of a wholly personal God everything depends on the acknowledgement, from the beginning, of One who, as God made Man, alone has direct access to God's inmost life. 'No man has ever seen God; but now his only-begotten Son, who abides in the bosom of the Father, has become our interpreter' (John 1. 18). The law could still be given through a man, one endowed with very special grace: Moses; for the law did not raise the question of access into the inmost life of God. But grace and truth, which are the blessings of Christianity, can only be imparted by the one Son who, abiding in the bosom of the Father, has first-hand acquaintance with the personal life and being of God (John 1. 17).

What God is in his personal life can only perfectly be witnessed in him. But man is not capable, and no creature is capable, of attaining to fellowship with God by his own efforts. Indeed, man with his burden of original sin is too body-bound to perceive purely spiritual realities. Only through the fact that God became man, and divine life was shown forth in a human form—through Christ alone, knowledge of God as a Being infinitely personal attained to a point of perfection that, humanly speaking, can never be surpassed. Whoever knows Christ, through personal contact and in loving faith, knows God (John 14. 9). Any other account of God by mere man, or by any other creature whatever, lags far behind the one given by Christ. The revelation of God's own life in Christ could and can only be transmitted by personal contact with him; it is only through trust in him that it dawns on the disciple what God is, and this gives him a surety for the truth of things he could not know by himself. As we said, this knowledge is not of course academic knowledge or any form of learning, but knowledge of salvation and of the right way to God through trustful recognition of Christ for what he is. That is why discipleship is of the very nature of Christianity. Christ is no teaching philosopher presenting notions formulated by himself and accessible to others under his guidance. Christ brings revelation, that is, he tells us about God's life as a Person. Such information could only be passed on in a personal account, and in its highest conceivable form only through him who is both God and Man. Therefore Christ is the supreme mediator through whom alone man can attain to God. It is sheer presumption for man to claim that he himself has found the best way to God— paganism never made such claims; and the man who considers that by his own powers he can discover well enough what God is in Himself, is setting himself above God and treating Him like something inanimate.

Surrender to Christ involves none of those limitations on the one hand, dangers on the other, that arise out of the nature of things when we have to do with a merely human master, subject to error and sin. As God, the very depths of each human soul are open to him by right, eternally, for all were made and redeemed by him. Therefore discipleship here should be without reserve, as of God himself. Indeed, only in fellowship with him can real surrender to God be accomplished, a surrender in which man renounces all self-assertion and thus acknowledges God to be God indeed. Humanly speaking, no one can be at home with God except through union with Christ. In communion with Christ, and through love for him, the disciple is so completely re-shaped by Christ's mind and Christ's action that these become the basis of his own life and he can rightly say, 'Christ lives in me' (Phil. 2. 5; Gal. 2. 19 ff.).

This bond is organic. It is so close, so vital, that it can be compared to a vine and its branches, to the head of a body and the limbs and other parts of it. A closer bond is inconceivable. The disciple remains in touch with Christ through all that is best in him, in his inmost heart of hearts he lets Him take charge, an act that reverberates through his whole being and lights up his whole life. Love for the Man who is Christ clears the way for that absolute acknowledgement which is the necessary prelude to knowledge of the absolute Being of God. Trustful familiarity has taught the disciple that he only apparently loses himself by his act of renunciation of self, for in reality that is the way he comes to himself.

So deep in a man does discipleship go that in time nothing is left unstirred by Christ's transforming touch. Nor is this the work of a stranger, still less is it the effect of a natural impulse: it springs from the very intimacy of love by which the disciple's inmost soul is ever more perfectly united to his Master's, so that Christ's influence on him has not only his full consent, but his active support through loving faith. Sanctification is the combined act of Christ and the disciple; pure grace on the one hand, which no one can merit, and on the other, full freedom. No other influences, of whatever kind they may be, can reach down to the inmost soul of man: and when a man is exposed to another sort of influence, the more external it is and remote from the heart of him, the more do grace and freedom diverge, and the less likelihood there is of a spontaneous response. For such an influence is liable to be possessive and assertive, wishing to force a total adherence. Authority on those terms towers over its subordinate as something impersonal and estranging, inimical to his freedom. No, Christ's redeeming love for man is the ideal model as well as the real model for all human authority; just as the loving submission of the disciple is what every form of obedience should aim at becoming, through inward transformation. Yet such is the imperfection of the spirit's hold on the body, here on earth, that an estranging element tends to creep into all forms of authority.

That is what is so new and so liberating in Christianity: that it is of its nature discipleship, incomparable discipleship in depth and width and height, a watershed for all else. Christianity has its own rules and regulations, but they are not the last word, nor do they force every-thing into their pattern. The rules and regulations of Christianity are themselves grounded in discipleship and personal relationship, and can at all times be frankly taken on by the disciples as their own, thus ceasing to be mere rules and regulations. If spirit and an attitude of mind could perfectly determine physical and external things without provoking resistance, no law would be necessary in Christianity. But since original sin came into the world, that is no longer possible. These things have a life of their own, which does not yield to penetrating and regenerating spirit without putting up some show of resistance. And penetration by spirit can only be done at some cost and not without conflict: in fact it takes a whole Christian lifetime to do it at all. The imperfection of physical inclinations is to some extent patched up by the law, which acts as a warning to Christians not to be led astray and do things which are incompatible with discipleship and can only damage it. But love should take the law more and more into its own hands and establish conformity, thus ridding it of its legal for-mality. Only the wholly perfect Christian could be wholly free from the law.

But to sinful man Christian freedom looks like compulsory service. By nature, he tends to consider freedom to be the possibility of giving free rein to selfishness and its hankerings. All too late he comes to see that he is merely bringing about his own perdition by falling into dependence on things of lesser worth, without being able of his own accord to free himself from his entanglements. The essence of finite, created freedom is the right to choose between good and evil, instead of merely acting by instinct like an animal. But the point is not, to take the course of evil, thus becoming involved in sub-personal levels of being subject to concupiscence, but to be capable of carrying out what is known to be good in spite of the resistance of the lower levels. And this brings with it a more perceptive sense of what is good and greater freedom to act in the light of this perception. Loyalty to accepted truth greatly increases the scope of freedom. But the lower levels have to come into line, and in so far as they offer resistance to the develop-ment of the person's true interests, they are condemned slowly and painfully to starve to death. Therefore it is, at first, only by faith that the new freedom can be apprehended.

Union with Christ works out naturally as fellowship among the disciples themselves. But the presence of Christ confers incomparable depth and power and the community of disciples possesses qualities which distinguish it from all other human groupings. In the Church—for this community is the Church—the spirit of Christ is ever living, and his presence is no less real than in the days of his earthly ministry. That is why all through the centuries the Church always put Christ in the foreground, the living Christ and his words, acts, attitudes and whole Being. In the Church's sacraments, her doctrine, directives and commandments, Christ is present in every age, ready with help for every age's special needs. He is far more than just a revered historic figure, like Plato or Buddha. And discipleship is a living reality at all times, always in direct contact with Christ himself through the Church. A Christian is not a disciple of the Pope's or of the Church authorities, but in obedience to them he is a disciple of Christ. All the love and reverence of Christians for the Church is directed to Christ himself, whom they find in the Church and through the Church.

But within the community the principle of discipleship continues to function. The right use of the sacraments, the deeper understanding and application of doctrine, the loving submission to Church guidance are continually being renewed by men who themselves, in an unusually perfect manner, are disciples of Christ, men who represent Christ more visibly and radiantly in their way of life and their whole being: the saints. Through them the living Christ appears in their own times and creates new forms of spiritual activity to suit changed conditions. But these very men, so highly endowed with grace, are the ones most conscious of being only disciples, so much so that they are not at all anxious to hold on to the people who come flocking to them. They are not masters, as they see it; each one of them asks nothing better than to betroth the people to Christ and bring the bride to the bridegroom (2 Cor. 11. 2; John 3. 29 ff.), rejoicing when one more soul has been won for Christ.

But each saint represents but a portion, a special side of Christ's abundance which is inexhaustible till the end of time—and represents it with a radiance of his own. This radiant portion, with the whole abundance in the background, is what disciples see who, through contact with the saint, have gained increase of intimacy with Christ. And they are animated by the same spirit, which becomes the basis of their life and work. They form a spiritual family bound together not by blood relationship but by that deeply seated relationship of a special kind, with Christ (Matt. 12. 48 f. ; Mark 3. 33 ff.; Luke 8. 21). A similar attitude of mind is likely to produce a similarity in the external conduct of life, and for saints this is not a matter of indifference, so close is their bond with Christ and so great is its informing influence. The outward form of life in such cases is the vessel within which the animating spirit is contained, for its greater protection and safety, for it is regarded as a precious heritage. Still, it is only as protective garb of the spirit and chosen attitude of mind that this outward form has any value. Where the spirit is lacking, it becomes mere dead husk, a burden and a self-deception. But even in this reduced state it still has a function: it can act as a warning, for the habit fosters the spirit. And it assures help and guidance when it is a matter of turning back to the original spirit. But one fact should not be overlooked: external things are much more subject to changing times than is the spirit, and it can happen that something that used to be an expression and clothing of the spirit has, through too obstinate adherence to custom without regard to changing times, turned into a strait-jacket, narrowing and confining in its effect. Time-conditioned as it always was, it must in course of time make room for something else that will be a better expression and support of the same spirit under changed conditions. It is all too easy and too stupid to go on believing that the spirit is kept alive by keeping on external forms, simply because these were reasonable and serviceable in given circumstances long ago. But equally, it is fanciful to suppose that in the human sphere the spirit can live on without the support of outward form.

When Christ's discipleship takes on a characteristic outward form out of loyalty to a saint—and this does not often happen—we have the beginnings of a religious Order. It is a way of life that grows out of the life, example, advice and teaching of the founder, and becomes a special kind of discipleship. An Order is to be distinguished from a sect, expressly and emphatically, by its awareness that it represents only one side of Christ's whole abundance, being but a particular reflection of it, only justified within the Church, which is the sole manifestation of the whole Christ. Thus, other organs of the Church will not be rejected or condemned for being different, and the Order's accepted view of Christ will not be proffered as the only valid one, to which all others must yield. Each Order came to its own characteristic form either because of the nature of its original mission or through pressure of circumstances at a given time. Even less than the saint does the more average Christian manifest the whole Christ, nor could he attempt to do so. But each, according to his situation in time and his special circumstances, feels himself drawn to one kind of discipleship rather than another. And here the question of vocation finds its solution—not the one affecting religious Orders in general, but the practical question of which Order to approach.

There are actually two main currents: the choice lies between the contemplative and the active life. Some are more gifted for work in transforming the conditions of human society, and feel themselves drawn to a way of life that gives useful outlet to these gifts. Others are by nature more inward-looking, submitting life and experience to the scrutiny of mind and spirit. These different attitudes are God-given, and are therefore not without bearing on the choice of a way of life, even if they alone cannot be decisive. The point is not that there are two mutually exclusive ways of life: that is not so, and we are only concerned with a personal preference for one or the other. One is not, from the religious point of view, better than the other. The idea that the contemplative life is of greater value in itself came from the Greeks and is closely related to the Greek philosophers' conception of God—Aristotle's in particular. Intellectual powers were looked upon as divine by the Greeks. God himself was described by Aristotle as pure perception. And intellectual perception was therefore considered the highest, 'the most pleasant and best', giving man a share in divinity. For here he is permitted, for a moment at a time, to enter into contact with what divinity possesses eternally and perfectly. Therefore the philosopher avoided physical work, which was considered inferior, and devoted his life to perception, to contemplation: this was reckoned as the highest form of life to which man could attain.

But for Christianity, it is selfless love of God and man that comes highest in the scale of human values (Matt. 25. 31–46), and is decisive; the greater and purer the love, the more worthy is the way of life or the act in question. For the crux of the matter is close intimate understanding with Christ and this is fostered by selfless activity no less than by contemplation. But when this love is lacking, both activity and contemplation lose their value equally (1 Cor. 13). Without contemplation, in the form of recollection, receiving the sacraments, and prayer of petition and thanksgiving—in fact all that composes the worship of God—acts are superficial and turn into mere selfish busy-ness, which has nothing to do with the Kingdom of God. For man cannot keep going in a world of Christian thought and values without making some sort of effort. It is only through the constantly renewed attempt to live up to it and conform more closely to the Christian standard, only through steady intercourse with Christ, that activity becomes transformed from within and fulfils its proper function, which is bringing men to act selflessly. If the effort is not made, then the egoistical undercurrents take command of the situation, and activity is misused as a means to gain favour and set oneself up as an object worthy of admiration.

The dangers of contemplation are no less great. Egoism can turn contemplation into a life of comfort and convenience, side-tracking all disagreeable intrusions. That constant testing by measuring up to reality may easily be omitted, and then contemplation degenerates into self-deception, vanity and pride. It is matter for thought that St. Ignatius of Loyola, who was a great man of prayer himself and an experienced guide of souls, came to the conclusion that of a hundred people devoted to prayer, ninety are deceiving themselves. Pious feelings are not enough for a transformation of being. We can say, 'Lord, Lord' without truly belonging to the Lord or deserving eternal life. Even the possession of exalted spiritual gifts is no surety that one does not belong to those who traffic in wrong-doing, whom the Lord disowns (Matt. 7. 21-26; 1 Cor. 13). Both ways of life presuppose a steady conquest of selfishness if they are to be pleasing to God and if love is to come to its full surrender.

At various points of history the saints are there as living models of what discipleship with Christ is, they are instruments of God bestowed upon the Church to rescue discipleship from degenerating into mere historicity and summon it back to be present in the present-day, thus keeping the Church alive and effective. The most perfect and effective disciple is one whose whole spirit and behaviour are alive in the present in all freedom. Only in the Church, with her sacraments and her saints, is it possible to be 'contemporary' with Christ in the way Kierkegaard rightly held to be essential for the Christian. But it cannot be done by trying to force history, or by denying it. To be present through a book is a diminished form of presence, and is insufficient for full discipleship. No one today can actually be a disciple of Plato's: to be his pupil is more possible. It is through the saints that Christ tackles the special troubles of every age, for through the saints initiatives are taken which the Church accepts and which find their final form and general validity as popular practices and customs or in directives and rules of the ecclesiastical authorities. Or else the spirit of the saints lives on in a religious Order and radiates into the Church through its life and works.

THE NEW MAN

That is a life-work for each and all. Through the grace of God and through the sacraments, each has received an inner character, dedicated to the Trinity, as child of God, brother of Christ, temple of the Holy Ghost, and this character each of us has to work at to make it more and more satisfactory and perfect, in the sphere of our own life. That utter submission without reserve which the creature owes its Creator, has become through God's love, revealed in his Son, a self-surrender in love. The man who feared to lose himself beyond retrieve under an obedience without reserve, now knows that it is in this personal act of selfless devotion that he finds himself and comes to himself at last. But it is a difficult thing to do. It does require of a Christian that he win through to perfect selflessness. But since, through separation from God, he lost part of the control of his body, man is by nature tied up within himself. In the place of spiritual spontaneity, it is the short-ranged physical impulse that asserts itself. And here lurks death. So man becomes engrossed in preserving his life, feeling all the while that it is doomed from the start. Hence the strained, cramped nature of his lust and greed, so unlike anything known to the animals. And this holding on tight to oneself is a great obstacle to pure self-surrender to God, in fact it makes it impossible for a man to recognize God as God, absolute and decisive centre of all life, it puts man as man in a false position in regard to God, and in regard to himself no less.

The overcoming of this self-centredness and the reconquest of the long lost lordship over the whole human sphere, are done through baptism, but not all at once. Baptism opens up the possibility and sets the point of departure. For, as we said, a man's self-surrender must be partly his own act, without in any way displacing God's creative act. God and what God created cannot be considered in relation to one another as though both were creatures: the creature is and lives and acts by the power of God alone, by the life that is bestowed on him moment by moment;—bestowed however in such a way that the creature is, through it, what he is: the person originally intended, and accordingly, freely himself. And, we repeat, it is in discipleship that grace and freedom are united—notions that appear incompatible to minds accustomed to think in terms of material things. The effort made to win a way through to God's will, within oneself and in one's environment, whatever the obstacles, makes self-surrender a reality. And it can only occur during a man's lifetime. It is meant as a progressive movement forward into the sphere of God's love in all its breadth and length and height (Eph. 3. 18). Due to human frailty and instability, the process has ups and downs and sometimes suffers collapse: a state of affairs which can only be remedied by God himself turning again with pardoning love. The inward strength of our love for God should steadily increase. The Christian should be able to encounter whatever occurs with growing simplicity and ease, seeing all things in the light of God and mastering and tempering them in the mind of Christ. Love should shine through the least happenings and doings of the day, nothing that is good and right in itself remaining outside its scope (Phil. 14. 8). 'In eating, in drinking, in all that you do, do everything as for God's glory', said St. Paul (1 Cor. 10. 31). The transformation involved is to be a complete one, of man as a whole, from the inmost heart of him to his activities outside in the world, and the whole process (with rare and wonderful exceptions) will unfold according to the constant laws of the spiritual life. It cannot all be done at once, and no steps can be omitted. It is, after all, a process of growth, one stage at a time, not like mechanical reconstruction. And we have to remember that the laws of the spiritual life are not like natural laws either, adamant and unequivocal, though they are often taken to be so. It is the inward attitude that is decisive for whether in a given situation the opportunities are rich or poor ones. A sudden stroke of grace—maybe a quite exceptional one—may in a moment put a man in a position he could otherwise only have reached by heavy going over years; the stories of almost miraculous conversions prove it again and again. But of his own authority a man can lay no claims to such grace, either for himself or for others; here he has to take into account all sorts of variations in spiritual development and formulate his requirements and give advice accordingly. When endeavours are directed towards achievements still beyond a man's powers, or unsuitable in his case, time is wasted and healthy growth endangered. Steady transformation from within in Christ, as lovers whose close intercourse and union of hearts makes them more and more alike—this alone is Christian living. As a man's clothing fits him and adopts his shape and characterizes him outwardly, so should the Christian put on Christ (Rom. 13. 14; Gal. 3. 27), in intimate union with him, displaying him to the world through his life. So he will be a new man, created in the image of God (Eph. 4. 24; Col. 3. 10), who can be taken into the boundless ocean of God's flooding, incandescent love, into the harmonious intercourse of Father and Son in the Holy Ghost.

That is the meaning, that is the aim of all Christian living. Every baptized man is called to the All-Highest. This vocation is a focus for earthly vocations. It is independent of a man's qualifications in philosophy or theology. Pure learning is not necessarily, as the neoplatonists believed, a stage on the way to God. The means to Christian living are equally accessible to everyone, and they are an inherent part of the vocation. Ever and again, invisibly visibly, we have the mysterious breaking through of this other-worldly vocation into our world through the sacraments, to call to mind our high duty, confer new graces and help us on our way. This the sacraments do at one and the same time: they render help, they present Christian living symbolically, and they anticipate its true end. Outwardly, there is no change; and yet the world is here torn open and transformed by a higher reality. Here we have for a moment, in the light of faith, the material world as it ought to be: an instrument, a means for revealing intrinsic truths and displaying God's powers. And so it is with Christian living. To the outward view it remains ordinary, often quite insignificant. And yet everything about it is penetrated with a radiance from within, from hidden depths, that totally transform it. By mysterious means, and yet quite plainly, Christian living is fed from new springs of life. And at times the super-worldly power within breaks through the mortal frame and radiates out into the world in all the splendour of God's glory. In the most sublime of the sacraments, the holy Eucharist, we have it all condensed: the transformation of the creature, union with Christ, utter self-surrender to God, and transfiguration as the fruit of this surrender.

And likewise in the saints the end of Christian living is realized, still imperfectly but nonetheless far beyond the average attempt. All are meant to strive for one-ness with Christ, becoming him, so that every thought, act and feeling—specially the latter, the hardest and the slowest of all—are so constituted, that Christ himself at that same place and in that same situation would have been of the same mind, and would have acted in the same way with the same feelings (Phil. 2. 5). This the saints achieve to a great extent—that a man be inwardly Christ's and Christ's mind radiate through the whole range of his life so powerfully, that without effort, premeditation, deliberation, or resistance, everything comes as it were straight from Christ's own heart, spontaneously, so that Christ could take it all on as though it were all his own, and could declare it to be so. That is what being a Christian means. The Christian is to be another Christ. The great task set is impossible of fulfilment. Impossible, and yet day by day, hour by hour even, to be tackled afresh. God once made a beginning for us in baptism, and what he did then lies outside the power of any created being; and he will one day bestow on our departure from this life the fulfilment no man can reach on his own account. But it is a fulfilment dependent on the loyalty and love with which a man tackles the job, so that it can be called his reward, although it is far more than any deserts of his could warrant, and is all due to the Father's kindness (Matt. 20. 1–16).

Through love man is made perfect, that is, like God. For God is love (1 John 4. 16). Only as Love is he one God in three Persons. For in this love the one Godhead is transmitted from Father to Son and from both to the Holy Ghost, in so perfect a manner that each Person is in full, equally perfect possession of the Godhead, but in the most personal way; so that the Father is not the Son, and neither are the Holy Spirit. God is perfect giving and receiving: they are in God equal. And this love has spread out in ever widening circles through creation and redemption, and has even brought to life beings that exist by it alone. Only eternal love is capable of creating in this fashion out of the void; for it alone needs no outside stimulus but acts as pure elemental generosity. If a man is capable of recognizing it, he should acknowledge it with love himself, and enter into the full stream of this current issuing from God. Like the sun withholding its rays from no one, but lighting and warming all alike (Matt. 5. 45), so is God's love shed upon all who enter its sphere, radiating love and life. It is no natural, perfunctory shedding of light, but freely willed. Just as God did not wait for us to love him but 'sent out his Son to be an atonement for our sins' (1 John 4. 9 ff.), so true love does not look for advantage or reciprocation. Wherever love can be, there it is to be found.

In perfect personal devotion to the threefold God, a man finds himself and is rescued from his self-estrangement. Devotion of one person to another is love, sheer love in the purest sense. And love makes a man complete and tends to his perfection. For in love a spiritual personality takes itself in hand, freely, and transposes itself into the centre of another, into the very hearth of another's life. To be able to give ourselves away we must first possess ourselves, and in performing this act of transposition we cannot let anything stand in the way. To love, one has to be. Perfect love is at once perfect self-possession and pure freedom.

Any form of self-estrangement is an obstruction to perfect love. Fallen man is however estranged from himself in many ways. There is a lot about him that is not, rightly seen, himself at all. All the levels of material, physiological and subconscious life are for his spirit difficult of access. Even in his conscious life much remains unlit. A man does not really know much about himself and his own motives. He often does not know what are the real sources of his actions and decisions. Seldom are they quite clear to him. That is why he is so insufficiently himself. And what he does not possess he cannot give away. Whatever about him is closed and impenetrable to himself cannot without grave risk open to another. If a man is estranged from himself, he is to the same degree estranged from his fellows and estranged from God. This self-estrangement can only be remedied if a man's spirit grow strong enough to penetrate into his own sub-personal levels and transform them from within, so that they offer no more resistance to the light, but rather, lit by the spirit, are set aglow and themselves shed light. A man's spirit has to grow so strong that it is no longer pulled down by the dead weight of his own sub-personal levels, its centre of gravity shifting to where he is no longer wholly himself. The lower levels must not be allowed to tug at his independence and hamper his spirit's mobility. But then it would be necessary for a man to drag himself up from his own depths by his own efforts. However, it is not only the burdensome load of his own sub-personal levels that baulks him here: the bottom of his being is not to be found in himself at all but in God; and only from God can the human spirit receive that inpouring of strength to transform his living body and make it really his own, transfiguring it, so that he can be complete with it.

But man as creature cannot dispose of God. Thus he never reaches his own bottom ground by his own efforts. So long as man is a stranger to God, he is estranged from himself. But love is the perfect remedy for unfamiliarity with God: it sets a man in God's very heart, to take part in God's own life. This own life of God's includes his creating and sustaining activity, by which all the world exists, by which each man exists. Thus by love of God, man bound to God takes part in his own creation and so comes to terms with his own ground. Only through God-given love of God is a man himself, and only thus can he establish contact with himself, till the last trace of estrangement disappears. In love, man is made perfect. The whole of Christian living has the function, by God's grace, of becoming more capable of this perfect love, winning through to great freedom, and without positively aiming at it nonetheless becoming more perfect.

Transformation, not elimination; a heightening of life, not death, is the meaning of Christian living. Notwithstanding that the first reaction of sinful man is to see it as pure negation and the killing of all that makes life worth living. Yet the motive force is not hatred of the body, nor is it longing to escape from the body as the soul's prison, escape from matter as from something unclean. All that God created is clean when it is handled with clean hands. And these clean hands are what Christian living is to restore. Freeing the body through the freeing of the soul is the real aim, and such a powerful penetration of the body by spirit that its life will be more alive, more mobile, healthier, stronger, more willing, more enterprising, and through the power of the renewed spirit will become immortal. Body must be wholly body with an unimpaired vitality proper to man, a man should be able to call his body truly his own. And matter itself should return to its original function through Christian living. Man is not to be freed from it as from something unworthy and unclean. It is to appear as what it is, God's creation. Things are to reflect God's light and thus reveal him and be themselves transformed; transformed, but remaining matter; and bodily life remaining bodily life, but letting the spirit shine through and willingly following the spirit in all respects.

A new attitude to reality, one determined by faith, is the effect of the new life. And a new relation to creation, with increasing power to gather all things into the one love of God. The new attitude to creation gives rise to a new perception of its reality, nearer to the truth. For unredeemed man sees things in a high degree as there for him, helps or hindrances as it may be, endorsing his existence or undermining his self-confidence. This way of looking at the world is the same as the animal's, a beast sees things either as potential prey or as potential danger, to the rest it is blind. The very fact that man is a spiritual being means of course that his range of vision is immensely greater than the animal's. But life's necessities induce somewhat the same way of looking at things: if things are there at all, they are there for him. And such exclusive concern with immediate needs means that if reality glimmers up from its depths, it is scarcely noticed. The spirit itself is scarcely noticed, as though it were wholly unimportant for physical life. Such a man comes up against reality as resistance to his plans: then it appears simply as an obstacle and barrier to the fulfilment of heart's desire. Yet when everything neatly falls in with heart's desire, a man lives in a sort of dream-world with a quite false idea of reality, until too late, when the plain truth emerges and he comes to grief. So we can see how a man's experience of the contrary nature of things makes him aware of their reality, and this is particularly true when people, not things, are concerned.

If a man can achieve a selfless attitude to the world, he will leave men and things to be what they are and do what they can do. Seeing their reality and their right to be themselves, and not only the advantages he can get out of them. Nor when they oppose him and fight will he immediately feel entitled to deprive them of their rights. He gives them their due, recognizing them for what they are intrinsically, even when their different way of being is obstructive to his own or damaging to his worldly prestige. A natural acceptance of things means that they are as though they were not there, for they are no longer regarded as things-to-be-used and remain first and foremost things-as-they-are. It makes a man appear clumsy; he ceases to be any good at looking after his own interests and is seemingly defenceless under attack, apparently in process of giving up the world and denying it.

But in reality this attitude makes him properly aware of the existence of men and things for the first time. Through apparent nothingness he attains to true fullness—as St. John of the Cross so earnestly insisted. He discovers how being on the watch for one's own advantage and constantly preoccupied with safety-measures covered a colourful abundance of creation with a grey film that made things uniform and dull, whereas now they shine out in the true splendour of their God-given diversity. New beauty opens up to him, a reflection and a faint foreshadowing of future glory for which all creation longs (Rom. 8. 19 ff.). Saints like St. Francis and St. John of the Cross proclaimed it. But the passage to this new day still passes through the night, the night of the senses and of the self-centred spirit, the night of renunciation, in which man lets his self-centredness wither away. The more it is his nature to confuse his true self with this self-centredness, the more bitter is the death of it. Only in faithful trust in Christ's word and example dare he risk the extreme wager of apparent self-abandonment. And yet only so will a man attain to perfection, fullness of being rid of all self-estrangement: in loving surrender to God he finds his way back to his own foundations, and by co-existing in the personal love of God he has them restored to him by grace. Thus he gains that very thing he so vainly strives for here on earth, and so perversely too as a rule. There is firm ground under his feet, he is no longer at sea, he is glad to be where he is and is at peace with what he is. His relinquished self is not lost like a drop thrown into the ocean but is fulfilled in the co-existence of love. Now at last he is wholly himself, when to be, in the fullest and highest sense, means, in all self-knowledge, to be free from the depths upwards, no more bewildered by darkness nor estrangement.

In God man is himself at last, himself in all his uniqueness. There exist false notions of divinity as the impersonal base and mystery of the world; and mistaking the self-seeking foreground ego for the true self also confuses the issue: thus the ascetical ideal has often been misrepresented as a self-renunciation by which the individual had to disappear as such in order to be a drop in the ocean of divinity. But this is practical annihilation and is, metaphysically, incompatible with the idea of individual personality. It would no longer be the person, with self-knowledge and self-possession, that would crown reality, but unconscious being, which, in the full sense in which we understand personality, is non-existent. But the theory does exist, and applies categories appropriate for material things to the most utterly personal relationship of all: to love between persons. Material things are mutually exclusive, not only in space but even more fundamentally, in their being. They can only be united and lose their separateness when one dissolves in another, leaving not two but one. And in reality this dissolution only takes place from one point of view, for the atoms of the drop that disappears in the sea remain as they were, atoms, or whatever the elemental unit of matter may be. However, that takes them beyond our reach. But the same is true of life: the units of being are mutually exclusive and remain indifferent to one another; knowing nothing of one another, like the plants, or very little, in a dull muddled way, like the animals. Bodily life knows union of a primitive kind, but only in a state of intoxication, when consciousness and individuality (it is held) are set aside. But this union is not a genuine one, nor in consequence is it a lasting one.

To be truly one is only possible to spiritual persons. They also possess the required mobility and the self-possession which permits them to enter non-spatially into the centre of another's being and to consider the world from that new angle, and with that other, and for him, to go out to meet it. Only when we come to the spirit do we encounter the possibility of being together and living for one another. But this being together, far from eliminating self-hood and individuality, rather brings them to whole-ness. Only in perfect love is man himself whole. And it is love, as we saw, that is the aim of Christian asceticism.

Certain pantheistic-sounding passages in the writings of the mystics can beyond doubt be ascribed to the use of terms belonging to systems of thought that described the first principle of the world as an impersonal one: their true meaning, however, was not pantheistic, but was intended to convey the rapture of union with God by means of a linguistic equipment insufficient for the purpose. But on the other hand we must not forget how the fact that man's spirit is bound to his body gives rise to a tendency to de-personalization, self-forgetfulness, and immersion in the impersonal. The history of religions proves it clearly. Orgiastic cults are to be found everywhere. But true religion has to overcome these aberrations, and above all the Christian religion, the only one that has not succumbed to the impersonal in trying to express the super-personal character of God. For in the revelation of the three-fold personality of the one God, man was given an answer to a question he often asked but could not answer himself.

Love for God causes streams of spiritual riches to flow to all the earth's bounds and beyond. It is the way man takes part in God's power of creation, giving without return. He becomes a source of highest spiritual life for himself and others. He is a unique and special rill from the eternal springs which are the source of his own love too (John 7. 38). No would-be inclusive conception of mankind, no general pattern of man covers him, blurring his individuality; he attains to the most exalted and pronounced individuality possible in all that is most truly, personally, himself. He is like God, too, who is unique and matchless beyond all conception. Love is open to all that is for as long as it is, for it is open, above all else, to the overwhelming and inexpressible greatness of divine love. Turned towards this, it grows—how, it hardly knows itself—but grows Godwards.

The point of asceticism cannot, therefore, be a promotion into universality by rejecting the body, supposing it to be the basis of human personality. This would mean relinquishing what is specific and merging into a cosmic indifferentiation. Nor can it be severing oneself from all sense-impressions on account of their intrinsically personal nature, in order to devote oneself to a purely intellectual world of abstract ideas. No, the outcome of asceticism should be seen as a positive endowment: that of becoming oneself once for all. For if man is truly unique, it is in his spirit rather than in his body. The higher they are in the order of being, the more increasingly various and more expressly unique are all spiritual beings. But in matter, at the lowest levels, specimens of the same species are no longer distinguishable from one another, so that one can replace another without any perceptible change in function. Then in plants, still more in animals, specific features are not only evident but play an increasingly important part. And men are specific and different from one another above all mentally and spiritually, whereas their physical needs and capacities are still very much alike. The limits of achievement in sport are very narrowly drawn, in comparison to all the possible degrees of intellectual and spiritual powers. And by means of the highest spirituality of all which is holiness, through self-surrender to God and disregard of the lures of cupidity, man imprints on human nature the most personal character possible, one and only of its kind. One glance at Christ and the saints suffices to show how true this is.

However, gain of individuality cannot be made an end in itself. Not because it is not worth striving for, not because it is of doubtful value; but because it is spirit, not object, and cannot and may not, therefore, constitute a field for the exercise of the will. The precious values proper to personality are attained only through dedication to what is objectively to be done. They grow as it were spontaneously into the right attitude and behaviour, but are latent at the point of issue of man's attention to things, and thus cannot be perceived objectively at all. Every attempt to objectify them is not only wholly contrary to their nature, but exposes them to egoism and its destructive onslaughts. Love and humility, perfection and humility are inseparable.

Owing to the clash between the efforts of bodily life on the physical plane and the endeavours of the spiritual life on its own plane, a clash which can to some extent be mitigated but never completely eliminated here on earth, Christian living appears in a peculiar double light. According to the point of outlook, it is seen now as the highest way of life, now as most bitter death; now as the gaining of selfhood, now as the loss of self. It makes the greatest possible demands on a man and requires of him such valour and heroism that all worldly valour and heroism are left far behind; and yet he is never accorded the honours and renown that are lavished on worldly distinction. Nor does he have that sense of satisfaction, nor that much-sought-after feeling of assurance and heightened self-awareness that honours and renown confer. True self-awareness is not dependent on such things as these and does not have to assert itself with an incessant I this, I that. So the man who is a Christian inevitably appears to be nothing special, a weakling rather than not, but nonetheless surprises by occasional signs of inexplicable power and a capacity for rising above common interests. To the man with no thought beyond the daily round, the living Christian is a mystery and provocation. Hence that odd mixture of respect and disdain with which he is regarded, which in people who have lost all sense of religion soon turns into superstitious fear and hatred.

This ambiguous aspect of the Christian life is not inherent. It is man-made and is due to his fallen and impaired freedom. Christianity as such is unequivocal. But its light breaks into different effects in different aspects of human life. There is no getting rid of the ambiguity, for indeed life and death are always present together; but death is a passage through and life is the enduring goal. This is clear in the New Testament. And in the lives of those true Christians, the saints, and in their paradoxical utterances. They groan in unutterable agony and lay claims to highest happiness. They admit their impotence and dereliction and yet their effect on many is transforming from the depths, and they bring to many new courage and new strength in facing life. They are not insensitive to pain, but no threats or martyrdom can deter them from pursuing their way. They are nearer to God than ordinary people, more securely borne by him, borne on his love, yet they endure the horrors and darkness of being apparently abandoned by God, until they are so purified that they can receive God's extraordinary gifts without harm, and the knowledge of being blessed with grace no longer trips them up and casts them down into greater depths, but can be accepted as a challenge to ever greater humility and self-surrender in love, empowering them to bestow God's graces on the world around them.

And all the other things that belong to Christianity: directives and establishments and ceremonies and customs, are all either forms and expressions of this love, or helps on the way to it, or protection against the dangers that threaten it. And that is their whole function. Dogma is God addressing man and making himself known to him in love. Faith accepts it in loving submission, admitting the limitations of merely human knowledge. The commandments forbid a self-centred attitude and propose a minimum standard of love for God and our neighbour, below which fellowship with God is lost and a man's true self is betrayed. Sacraments are the points where the love of God incarnate enters our world, in physical guise, to help make the earth holy, and as an outward sign of the invisible effect they have within us and of the end to which they are intended to bring us in course of time. At least a beginning of loving submission and surrender, renouncing the crassest forms of self-love, must animate Christian living, and Christian worship too, if they are to be truly Christian. On the other hand, God's grace and God's love are beyond human comprehension: he does not extinguish the flickering wick nor break the trembling reed; but takes pity on the merest effort, lovingly nursing it to life.

His love summons all to perfection, so much so that a sectarian Church of intolerant saints has never accorded with it. His Church is the Church of the many, of the ordinary people, among whom, unknown to themselves, least known to themselves, the extraordinary ones emerge, those with a passionate, consuming love for Christ. Their glow makes even the tepid warmer, and indeed any warmth there is among them is due to the consuming fire of Christ's love.

Those are the lines of Christian living, and all those great important sides of life which man rightly takes so seriously must come into line with it: material possessions, relations between the sexes, and the ordering of society. As a man's attitude to all these becomes more satisfactory, his love for God and man will become increasingly pure, and he will rise to being more and more perfectly himself. His own depths are not directly accessible to a man and cannot be the object of exertions of will-power. But through his behaviour towards the world of men and things he can by reflex action work at his own transformation. That is why it is so important that behaviour should be right, leading on to true love.

Now human behaviour in general takes two forms, determined by the special vocation of each individual man: ownership, or poverty; marriage, or chastity; social freedom, or obedience. The end is always the same, perfection through love; but the ways to it are different. We shall now examine how these different ways lead to the same end, and why the way of poverty, chastity and obedience, which can never be the way of more than a small number, has a special connection with Christianity. But as both ways, unlike though they may be up to the penultimate stage, meet at the final goal, they are not indifferent to one another but are there for one another, for mutual help and support.

CHAPTER TWO

Possessions and Poverty

PROPERTY AND SELF-FULFILMENT

CHRISTIAN living brings a man into possession of himself by the fact that he assigns himself to God by being a disciple of Christ's. But that is not what he means by ownership and property. Property is more likely to be a covering term for the whole gamut of things he can dispose of as he likes, where no one else has any rights and intrusion can be countered, forcibly if required. Property only exists where men are. The animal makes no such claim to material things beyond its immediate needs. This is very remarkable, for the need for property obviously depends on the requirements of physical life. Man needs food, clothing and shelter in order to exist. But that is not all: his spiritual life is bound to his body, and he needs material things to cultivate his mind and spirit as well as his body, things that he shapes to his own ends and that constitute his culture. Man, unlike the animal, is never content with nature alone, everything he touches bears the stamp of his spirit. So property is dependent on man's spiritual and physical nature. As such it is no purely natural phenomenon.

Thus man creates his own world in nature, building on natural foundations. This world is the expression of his spirit and the assertion of his self-possession. For only as an independent being at peace within himself can he face up to nature and competently address himself to his creative activity. He has his property at his disposal and can thus venture to propose ends that are not yet in evidence; he can transfer his energies and use natural resources to divert the course of things and make them follow his plans. Human culture is an expression of man as such, it expresses his spirituality and independence, but it also tells of his indigence and subordination as body-soul compound. Power and predicament: the paradox is inherent in human culture. It depends on man himself which tendency will be uppermost. The paradox is further present in the influence of cultural things on men's relations to one another. They facilitate contacts as exponents and stimulants of men's minds. Speech is not possible without sound, nor expression without body: in the same way ideas, attitudes, choices become widely known through the works which they induce, through books, and art of all kinds for instance. Cultural things promote human intercourse, an essential element of more advanced cultures. They bring men together and foster social life.

But in so far as they are material things, they tend on the contrary to separate men. Material things are mutually exclusive in space. They stand in the way, and this produces physical reactions which reverberate into the very soul of man. A material thing can be used for one purpose only at any given time, simultaneous functioning is out of the question. But it is not enough for a thing to be available only at the time it is functioning. Man's self-consistency in time makes him able to foresee today what he will do tomorrow and to lay his plans far ahead. But to carry them out he needs the assurance that all necessary adjuncts will be at hand at the right moment, and that no one else shall deprive him of the fruit of his labours, however delayed. The way to meet the situation is of course to cut other people out and see that they remain out. Thus a thing is a man's property when it is permanently available to him and to him alone.

Moreover this picking and choosing of things and removing them from common use is a form of self-expression as well as of self-defence. A man knows himself to be different intrinsically, as a person, and can set bounds between himself and all the rest; and by the same process he can put a fence up and claim what is inside it for his own. His self-possession extends to the world about him, and the more there is, the more expansive does he become and the more self-assertive. Wealth displays a man's personality and power, that is why it is called his *means*. Whoever has means is in a position to make his mark on the world, and by taking thought and using natural resources wisely, he can extend the range of his activities almost indefinitely.

Property guarantees personal autonomy and independence from other people's encroachments. The proprietor is sole lord and master, other people have no admittance. Thus property becomes a bastion of freedom against arbitrary action from outside. Here a man has a sphere of his own safe from attack, and he needs such a sphere: his body has many needs and makes him dependent on a number of material things. If they are removed, he is exposed to hunger, suffering and death. Thus his freedom is exposed too, for it is dependent on the conditions of his bodily life. In order to steer clear of suffering man is tempted to yield to demands he would normally reject. But if a man has sufficient wealth to parry attempts to force his hand, his freedom is secured and no one can tamper with it.

These are important functions of property: to serve as expression and defence of personal autonomy. The fact that man is so largely made up of his body means that this double function is no matter of chance. Property is one of the ways a man exercises and develops his freedom and creative powers, and all this is essential to self-realization. So he is proud of his wealth, it reflects what he is and what he can do, it enables him to subdue nature and carry his weight in the world of men. It constitutes the most outward, visible and tangible manner in which a man can make himself felt in the world about him.

Property would appear to be the indispensable means for a man progressively to become himself. It alone secures freedom from outside attacks. Moreover through his body a man occupies space in the world of matter, and he cannot do without it; thus he only attains to himself by activity, transforming the world by the power of his mind and making it serviceable to his own ends; and by dint of measuring up to the resistance of matter he confirms and increases his own personal powers. Thus things become his. Thus the capacity to hold property and the right to do so is intrinsically linked to human personality.

THE MAMMON OF INJUSTICE

It seems clear that an increase of wealth means a corresponding increase in the value and dignity of the human person. And that is what people naturally believe. The notion even affects their idea of God. Man always pictured divinity in terms of extravagant wealth, the mainspring of all property-holding. The heathen accompanied their prayers with costly and magnificent gifts and entreated the gods to bestow wealth upon them, for influence, esteem and power follow in its wake.

The scandal was all the greater when Christ, the Son of God made Man, appeared on earth in utmost poverty. He was God present in human form: surely, as image of the Father, like him in all respects, he should have made a display of wealth and splendour in his human life, for how could God be poor? The poverty of Christ seems to put man's dignity and freedom in question. Unless of course it were to have a deeper meaning, hidden from natural man.

This meaning is clear to us only when we recollect that release and expansion of personality are only one effect of property. Just as much and just as immediately, we discover in it necessity and coercion. For man's bodily needs throw him back upon material things and tie him to them, and thus harsh necessity holds him in its grasp. His elemental needs make imperious demands, urgent ones. They cannot be put aside like cultural activities, which can wait. Matter cannot wait without ceasing to function. Man must expect at any moment that the material side of life will clash with his own schemes and interests. And he cannot let it just run on either, not for any length of time, he has constantly to be on the look out for all sorts of contingencies, ready to spring to action. If it all gets to be too much for him, he becomes so engrossed in his worries that he hardly has time and energy left for the things of the spirit, that is to say, for a proper human existence.

Man succumbs to this danger in two diametrically opposite ways: too great poverty for the large majority of men is an insuperable obstacle to a worth-while human life. Whoever has to spend his whole time and energy on providing for the barest necessities, suffering hunger and lack of shelter, has little inclination for spiritual values. And he is in great danger of becoming servilely dependent on others and losing his inward and outward freedom and with it his self-respect.

But too much property is also dangerous. A man keeps himself busy running it and adding to it, and it may well happen that this preoccupation takes full possession of him. Thus he no longer belongs to himself but becomes the property of his property. Thus he becomes estranged from himself and is just as little free as the all-too-poor man. Willy-nilly he has to meet the claims his property makes on him. As his wealth increases, so does his fear of losing it. For wealth is not only a defence against outside attack; it also offers a far wider field for possible onslaught. In his possessions it is a man's self that is vulnerable, because his property is an extension of himself in the world. Thus it can come to a complete reversal of the proper relations between man and property. His possessions confine a man's aptitudes to anxious concern for his property and the true human values are done to death.

Then, property is apt to become coercive in relations with other people, and most of all in those respects in which it is supposed to be security and safeguard for freedom. It can only become so by exclusive action. The result of this is division and separation. One cannot keep people off one's property without keeping them away from oneself. One cannot exclude them from things without excluding them from one's own life. One can hardly defend one's own freedom at all without infringing that of someone else by withholding goods necessary for his livelihood. To increase the scope of one's own freedom is to diminish that of others. Equally, every increase of another man's property is a potential threat to one's own autonomy. It is not simply a matter of having enough possessions but of possessing more than the other man in order to anticipate and forestall any potential menace. When the other man adds to his means, it looks like injustice even when it is not done at one's own personal cost. Envy and ill-will accompany his success. But everyone has an interest in forestalling a threat from outside and a man will multiply his possessions in order to do so more adequately, thus becoming himself a potential danger to others. So there arises a great competition in amassing wealth, a limitless competition swelling to monstrous proportions because of man's inherent spirituality.

The desire for property is perverted into a senseless striving for more and more and more. Property is a function of society—and it becomes a source of hatred and envy. Property ought to bring men together and it divides them in bitter enmity and gives birth to the diabolical desire to damage the other man, even when nothing is to be gained from it. And this occurs not only among individuals but among groups and whole nations. Atrocities, murders, wars and the devastation of entire cultures are the outcome of this diseased will to possess and they bring destitution and misery into the world far in excess of any happiness and prosperity that wealth can account for.

This perversion of property, all too clearly demonstrated throughout the whole history of mankind, this unquenchable and measureless desire to possess, points to a still deeper human perversion. When once a man possesses as much as he can reasonably make use of, one would suppose he would leave it at that and take time off to enjoy his acquisitions. But this he does not do and then he feels he is missing something; he has a hope that he will come upon it in further accumulation of wealth relentlessly pursued, but he hopes in vain. In fact unredeemed man demands much more of property. He rightly sees it as the expression and safeguard of his individuality but all the time he is conscious that his existence is under threat, and it appears to him that an increase of property is the best way to eliminate his sense of insecurity. Under the influence of his body and its urge to objectify everything, man explains himself to himself not directly, *sui generis*, but in a roundabout way, in terms of the world, and thus he tends to the opinion that his whole existence, so understood, has to be maintained and promoted by the world. He overlooks the fact that the mere ability to project himself into the world presupposes the existence of a self. He forgets that you can only secure what is already there, you can only nourish what is already alive. No amount of feeding can make a dead thing live, it can only preserve life, and property cannot produce freedom if it is not already there from some other provenance. If man's existence had no inherent flaw it would be exposed to no menace from outside.

Man is a victim of the error that his existence is his own to hold and protect by ever greater extensions of control over material conditions. The ineluctable frailty of man is seen not where it truly lies, but instinctively projected into the world and that is where he tries to deal with it. He is driven by the lash of fear to go on feverishly adding to his gains. Yet each new gain proves a disappointment because it does nothing to remedy the sense of anxiety which overhangs all human ownership. And he ends up in a whirlpool.

The more he is lashed by anxieties and focuses his individuality and the whole meaning of his existence on the acquisition of wealth, the more does he identify himself with matter. As such, matter is sealed up in itself and indifferent to anything else. It has its own laws and follows them regardless of what may happen. It is hard and heavy and alone. But what is natural to matter in relation to its order of being, is fatal to man. He ceases to be really man. From time to time it crosses his mind how senseless all his efforts are and he catches a glimpse of the abysmal void within him. At this he falls into despair and tries to rid himself of unwelcome visions by means of increasingly agitated activity. He grows hard and insensitive to the suffering of his fellows and finds himself more and more solitary. His heart grows colder and colder, freezing in the arctic seas of egoism.

Now the desire for gain takes on such measureless proportions because its deep roots lie in the relation of man to his Creator—a relation damaged by sin. Man is no longer conscious of emerging directly out of God's hands and being borne on God's hands from moment to moment. He no longer knows how the fragility and vulnerability of his own being is only the reverse side of the loving will of God who bestows life on him freely and maintains it freely too. Therefore he does not ascribe his incapacity to Him who alone can be alone and from whom all created things come. He cannot turn trustfully to God and experience the love of God which is all generosity. He is convinced he has to attend to the stability and security of his existence himself, and to do so he turns instinctively to material things. They are, no doubt, he thinks, the easiest to manage. But it is an enterprise which is doomed to failure and fear seizes hold of him and drives him on to those demoniacally disproportionate efforts. If he stops exploiting his self for a single moment, he feels he is plunging headlong into the void. He has great expectations of being granted wealth, success and influence by the worldly powers he idolizes. Yet at the same time he tends to consider matter as something evil and to condemn it as the origin of all evil, partly because he feels it to be a burden and a shackle on his freedom. Even in pagan days efforts were made to be rid of the burden in order to live a carefree life.

Property has now become a separating wall between man and man, and between man and God too. The whole conception of reality is perverted. The independence and invulnerability proper to man in his material existence are mistaken for an absolute stability of existence based on itself and in no need of a Creator. Man's material existence is thus taken for his real existence, and spiritual and divine life look quite unreal beside it. A man sees his property as a means to making that stability his own.[1]

Practical materialism is one of the great recurrent temptations to which fallen man is liable. But if man could of his own powers see to the bottom of material being, he would find Him there who is both Author and Lord of it all. Everything in the world would be seen as a revelation of his love and a reflection of his beauty and power. And he would draw a sense of security and trustfulness from the presence of this goodness and splendour: he who so lavishly endows lifeless things would not be niggardly and mean when it came to man (Luke 12. 28; Matt. 6. 26–30), and he could well cease to worry about his existence, knowing it to be secure in the Fatherly hand of him who is the Author of all things.

But fallen man does not find this attractive. Since his mind and spirit lost contact with their mainspring, his capacity for being himself has dwindled even in relation to the world. All his efforts to overcome this weakness only increase it and make it more unbearable. Within himself man finds no firm ground left on which to take his stand, for he has turned away from his true ground. He is overpowered by the things of this world and succumbs to their false promises. But the things are not responsible for this: man in his anxiety projects his mirage onto them and more or less deliberately deceives himself.

In anxiously turning to outward goods for the foundation and sup-

---

[1] Cf. J.-P. Sartre, *L'être et le néant*, Paris, 1943.

port of his very existence, man becomes a stranger to himself. He sees the heart of the matter in material things, he measures himself by the size of his property and wants others to esteem him accordingly. Thus he situates his most intrinsic self in something that is not himself at all and never can be. For no possessions, not even things shaped by human hands and human skill, allow for a transforming penetration into the very essence of matter: things remain wholly external. The whole achievement of man in the shaping of cultural things consists, as a physical act, merely in the rearrangement of things in space. Man can go no further in the attempt to influence matter directly. Matter is something fundamentally alien to him and quite indifferent to its manipulation for cultural purposes. Man cannot change the laws of matter. Alien it is and alien it will remain. There is no means of making the things we use completely our own. Nevertheless man believes that through the prolonged existence of certain things he can provide himself with a prolonged existence too, a future and a settled centre. He measures his opportunities by his property as his means, his substance.

Thus man's future would lie in matter and matter has no future in the real sense. He looks for opportunities in something inert and incapable of doing anything except being what it is at the moment. He sees himself in what has no self and is far below him in the order of being. Thus he is truly lost and has no idea that property can only be the product of a spiritual power and is only then property. He misunderstands himself and is spiritually far removed from himself. Hence the emptiness and dissatisfaction. It was a great mistake of Marx's to consider that necessity and insufficient means of subsistence alone estrange a man from himself, though poverty and freedomless dependence can certainly do so, for man is only himself through freedom, situating the centre of his being in spiritual things and living out of that centre; and excessive anxiety about sheer necessities makes such a life very difficult for ordinary people, if not impossible. But property and an untrammelled lust for possessions are equally calculated to make a man a stranger to himself. Therefore a civilization that only lives for economic values is inhuman and man gets lost in it, it is an unhappy, discontented civilization with the germ of death in it.

Such is the state of affairs since the Fall: in all unredeemed ownership there lurks a certain godlessness, a hatred of one's fellow men and an estrangement from oneself; all property is more or less 'base wealth' (Luke 16. 9). In property, fallen man seeks a guarantee for his existence, but only God can give him this. So wealth is set up in the place of God

(Luke 12. 16–21). In his anxiety he takes all sorts of steps to exclude the other man from his precious property and hates him as a potential rival whose very existence is a menace to undisturbed enjoyment of his wealth. Property cannot open and expand the heart, it hardens and closes it. Man is become like his idol, matter. Like matter he knows but one means and one power: the relentless exercise of force, and gives himself up to it, having recourse to violence when he is the stronger and fawning slavishly when he encounters one more powerful than himself.

With no firm base within him, how was he to resist the suction of the lust for possessions? Only a divine power coming to him freely as grace could save him, only a redemption. Only borne on the wing of renewed powers could he become capable of possessing without being possessed by things, capable of making them his own without succumbing to them, capable of raising them up to himself instead of being dragged down to their level. This redemption has come to man through Jesus Christ. As God incarnate he has shown people the truth about God, and about earthly possessions and their worth, and told them how their relationship to both can be put right. But those who have hitherto taken wealth for an effect and pledge of divine favour are scandalized to discover that what is meant is the extreme poverty in which Christ lived.

RELIGIOUS POVERTY

With Christ a new evaluation of earthly property came into the world. When natural good sense says, with the pagans, 'Blessed are the rich', the new attitude was: 'Woe upon you who are rich; you have your comfort already. Woe upon you who are filled full; you shall be hungry' (Luke 6. 24 ff.). And on the other hand: 'Blessed are you who are poor; the kingdom of God is yours. Blessed are you who are hungry now; you will have your fill' (Luke 6. 20 ff.). Thus beatitude comes first (Matt. 5. 2). To the rich young man in search of perfection, the Lord said: 'In one thing thou art still wanting; sell all that belongs to thee and give to the poor; so the treasure thou hast shall be in heaven; then come back and follow me' (Luke 18. 23).

How was this possible? Christ was after all God in human form and human behaviour. Is God not rich? How can the possession of the things he created be a curse? A God who is poor and loves poverty is not in good taste, according to Nietzsche. But the poverty of Christ is there as a fact that cannot be swept aside. It was no accident—that was even more impossible in his life than in any other human life— for it accompanied him from the manger to the Cross. It was intentionally there as an intrinsic element in his life, and it is not due to incompetence or impotence. The miracle of the multiplication of the loaves, the changing of water into wine at the Cana marriage feast, showed that one word would have sufficed to provide our Lord with all the wealth of the world. But that word remained unspoken.

Poverty is required of his disciples too, of those who want to follow him. It must therefore be a means to perfection and, at a deeper level, in a mysterious way a representation of the nature of God.

That is in fact the meaning of Christian poverty. It is meant to bring man into the right relation with earthly things and break down the wall he has built up between himself and his fellows and between him and God. Freed from the spell of riches, man is able to contemplate worldly goods with an impartial eye, they are now truly his own in quite a different way. He will recognize where true wealth is to be found and will at last achieve what he was struggling for in vain, so long as he was concentrating on earthly things: fullness and perfection, freedom and security.

First of all he needs to be transformed through and through. The redemption of man by Christ is the starting-point and gives him new powers. But after that saving act at the heart of him that sets him off, he has to work at his own liberation with the help of God's grace. The goal of perfect freedom lies at the end of a weary struggle, and this struggle is a matter of duty and obligation for all Christians. None is exempt who hopes for salvation. There is however a choice of two ways of setting about it.

If matter and earthly property were bad in themselves, man would have no alternative but to renounce them altogether. But it is not material things that are evil, they are made by God. The source of evil lies in man. Man must turn to God anew. In redemption through Christ and through union with him, light and power are his. With their help he can approach earthly property as Christ wishes it to be approached; seeking for the final prop and meaning of existence no longer here but in God. In his inmost soul he will be free from possessions, for he has the knowledge that they belong to his outward sphere of life only, and have but a subordinate function in human life, however much they may press their claims. As all being comes from God, the being of things too, and is outside human comprehension, man comes to realize that he is only here as warden and authorized agent of God and will act accordingly. It is God's will that property be a means for the development of personality, of which the final perfection is selfless love for God and man. Troubles and losses should make man aware of how instability is the mark of earthly things and, rather than goading him on to more and more breathless anxious acquisitiveness, turn his heart to God who alone is worthy of his trust. Now this state of anxiety in which man lives constantly gives rise to a false conception of riches, so there is no truce and no peace in the war he has to wage. But from the heart of battle there emerges a new sense of inner peace and an assurance that is not of this world.

The Christian struggle for freedom is really a hard one. Property makes so many claims on a man, he has to be on his guard all the time to keep it within manageable bounds, or he will find himself indulging in arrogant egoism, looking down on his fellows disdainfully, or taking up a sham I-stand-alone attitude—chronic temptations that threaten to drag him down for good and all. No wonder that a man who has learnt from Christ's example and found encouragement in it grasps at a surer means of securing freedom, embracing Christian poverty in the strict sense. It is not just a way of getting rid of one's worries, though there is no property-holding without cares attached, as the heathen philosophers knew. But first, it is an incentive for a man to restore order of the right kind in his own life and in his relations with God and his fellows. To be more of a man and more truly a man, as complete and perfect a man as possible: that is the purpose of Christian poverty.

It is not enough to rid oneself of a dominating concern for amassing wealth; Christian poverty takes on an appropriate positive form too: once the high decision has been made, the evil has to be tackled at the roots and the perverted will-to-property be deprived of everything that might possibly give it scope. Man cannot entirely cease to need things. And to use things is no evil in itself. Possessions are only dangerous on account of the egoism that seems inseparable from them and the abuse of them for selfish ends. It is checkmate to self-will when a man has nothing left for his own personal use. And the ensuing state of dependency leaves egoism without a foot to stand on. That renunciation is truly and deeply meant is proved by the fact that the number of things used is reduced to those strictly necessary for carrying out one's obligations. Observe that a man is not to be impoverished to the extent that he becomes less capable of imparting spiritual instruction, for instance. But the greater his spiritual power and freedom, the further dare he go in the matter of renunciation.

His state of dependency in regard to the things he uses is there to anticipate any tendency to cling to things perversely and deprive others of them needlessly. The community is property-holder and control is done through its appointed representative. In this way things are put back into the service of Christian love again. But his state of dependency is chiefly valuable in arousing a new acceptance of the fact that all things are always given to us by God; independence through worldly possession is illusory and not in accordance with ultimate truth. We are masters only as creatures, and creatures are those on whom things are bestowed in order to be used in the sole service of the Creator. There is no self-deception in the belief that we have already gained our freedom from things when it is linked to dependence on a man: renunciation hurts, and thus keeps us in mind of how our attachment to things persists. The head of the community has charge of the allocation of things for use and thus becomes the visible representative of God and his benevolence. His obligations are no less arduous than those of his subordinates. To be a living model of God's fatherly liberality is not easy, giving freely and selflessly as far as is good and profitable, as far as love of God and man is thereby fostered. He cannot abuse his position by taking life comfortably and keeping the best for himself. Nor is he the owner, but only God's administrator responsible for the distribution of things, just as the others are responsible for the use to which things are put.

Poverty shatters the false security based on property. The first effect on the natural plane is an increased sense of anxiety. For a man to set aside all the props that means and property put at his disposal, to throw off the esteem and influence they brought him, in order to make do with barely enough for his immediate needs, is to all appearances to cast himself into the void. What about security for the future? That apparent dependability of material goods gave him a sense of having a hold on the future. Who will now save him from hunger and destitution? But above all, how is he to get his own way and thus to be himself and develop his personality? The effect of renunciation looks at first like a new greater dependence, the dependence of enforced poverty which cannot as a rule be expected to raise and liberate a man. Indeed, renunciation is only salutary when it is borne on trust in God's goodness and when it is truly undertaken out of love of God. It must issue from the certainty that God does not abandon his own but cares all the time and prepares what is best; a natural acknowledgement of God is not enough. It gives faith in Christ, it provides the unshakable conviction that Christ's teaching and Christ's example are unconditionally and without exception authoritative for us because he is God's Son, and because as Man his manner of life was such that true divinity was given bodily form and expression. The love of the Father was revealed in Christ, the Father who cares for man and who is not too exalted to look after him—and not only him but the most humble things in creation too: the lilies in the field and the sparrows on the roof (Luke 12. 22 ff.; Matt. 16. 25–34). He so ardently desires man's salvation that he gave his only Son for it (John 3. 16). The watchful fatherly love of God was revealed in Christ and in his poverty. Voluntary poverty takes all its directives from this fact and seeks to give life its appropriate outward form too, in accordance with what it knows of the love of the Father, which is the gift of faith. With the assurance that Christ's way of life is the expression of the divine life and that it cannot be surpassed, it is adopted as model. Christ's life shows that renunciation is no real impoverishment but is the way to attain to goods of a higher order which fallen man had lost sight of.

Christian poverty is only possible and only achieves its purpose if it lives by faith in Christ and love for him, and if redeemed man comes through Christ to realize that man does not live by bread alone. Only with this complete trust in Christ can a man dare to venture out into the apparent void which lack of possessions means to his natural understanding and to his provident instincts. Otherwise he falls into a new and much worse predicament. When a man has adopted poverty, he will take daily action to keep alive his trust in God, and from the constantly reiterated confirmation of this trust he will draw nourishment for his love of God. He will accustom himself to accepting all things as from the hand of God, he will know that God's hand is always open at the right time (Ps. 144. 15 ff.).

But this is no longer as apparent as it was before the Fall, now it requires an act of faith. It is dark knowledge and to man's natural understanding, which is so essentially materialistic, it is without foundation. From this point of view, renouncing a security based on earthly goods looks like a leap into the void. And the more a man has hitherto expected to find himself in earthly goods, the more crazy does poverty appear, as a giving up of one's self and a loss of personality. Awareness of the presence of God in things no longer takes the form of trustful confidence and pure joy, but mostly springs into evi-

dence only in the pain of relinquishment. It is a very direct pain with
the whole force of reality behind it; the presence of God appears in
comparison shadowy and unreal. The idea that security can be found in
wealth has to be given up *before* it is replaced in any perceptible way
by another form of security.

The way back to oneself is through apparent loss of self, through
death and negation. Only in the power of Christ's grace and in loving
faith in him and his word can a man resign himself to going through
this apparent negation. To natural man, renouncing, and inwardly
relinquishing the will to possess, seems to be as utterly impossible as
that a camel should pass through a needle's eye (Matt. 19. 24; Mark
10. 25).

The exposure and pain of privation are there continually to remind
us that man is not in command of things and cannot possess them
utterly. It ought to make him attentive to the fact that they come from
God and belong to him alone, and are available to man only to help
him do his duty. Egoism accepts all life's gifts as a matter of course,
and this is the only way it can gradually be curbed. In its place comes
a sense of grateful wonder that all we need is always there, that earth,
sun and moon and stars, men and animals and plants are all around us
and serve us faithfully. The delusive haze which egoism casts over
everything becomes progressively brighter and more transparent.
The insecurity of poverty reminds us all the while that things are not
there on their own account nor do they lie in our power—their
intrinsic being eludes our selfish greedy acquisitiveness—they are at
each moment renewed by God. But chiefly it makes a man's fundamental attitude of mind sound and well again. For he is wrong to seek
his point of gravity in his physical and emotional life, it lies elsewhere, in
his personal existence founded in God, which only attains to fulfilment
through yielding itself up to him. Anxiety dissolves in trust in God
and love for our neighbours becomes a workable proposition. Security
measures based on private property become increasingly superfluous
as man puts his whole trust more and more in God's love. Possessive
greed dies from the roots upwards. There is no desire left for more than
is necessary for life and its obligations. Everything else is for our
fellow men. And the economic value of things is undoubtedly increased when they are available to everyone to whom they can be of
service. And this leads to an increase of general joy. My fellow is no
longer my rival who might rob me, and my fear of him abates. This
removes a great obstacle on the way from man to man. Now hearts

can open to love: concern for things no longer forbids it. Earthly goods are once more capable of mediating and expressing love. Thus Christian poverty lives on love of God and love of man as neighbour, and waxes to ever greater maturity. Indeed it is a singularly effective means to perfection. Christian poverty makes men into images of him who lets his rain fall on the just and the unjust (Matt. 5. 43 ff.). The truly poor man is one who wants to share, to help, to give; to give out of the wealth of divine love which is poured out in his heart, to give earthly goods as bearers and interpreters of this love which has taken him on and folded him within its flood.

The meaning of poverty is, after all, freedom from possessive greed. Lack of possessions does not automatically produce this freedom, and exposure and material privation do not yet constitute perfection. Indeed it is not really a matter of living exposed, still less of living in filth. Notwithstanding, the capacity to accept exposure is the touchstone of inner freedom. It is easy to sit in an armchair in a comfortable room and rave about poverty romantically and unrealistically. Christian poverty is not concerned with the romance of the simple life; this may even be a refined form of self-seeking.

It is good for things to be used, but not for motives of self-satisfaction. If a thing is necessary and useful to the service of God and our neighbour, let us go ahead and put it to that use. A certain reluctance to go to great expense or to install modern equipment when it would really be of great service, is not necessarily a sign of the spirit of poverty. It may be; there is always the danger of becoming too deeply involved and it is a sure instinct to feel that mechanization tends all too easily to rob human relations of their personal character and make them too technical. And this poverty has to oppose at all costs. Technical proficiency must never be allowed to run independently and follow its own weight, it must remain subordinate to personal considerations. Where it protrudes too markedly into human relations, the gift is no longer a gift in the full sense and loses its efficacy. It is of course a different matter when helpful equipment and mechanical means for simplifying work are turned down out of indolence or a sort of manicheism which envisages matter and technical things as intrinsically evil.

But to aim at settling down and living comfortably is not in accordance with the spirit of poverty. When freedom from care for earthly possessions becomes a good excuse for letting oneself go, then poverty has turned into its opposite. For most people, the need to earn their livelihood is what chiefly spurs them on to work. Poverty effects a substitution: it replaces one motive by another. For work on those terms leaves a man little scope and tends to make a slave of him. But poverty stresses the spirit and value of work, which should act as a more effective spur than merely life's necessities. To perceive its true value is to keep work within proper limits when it threatens to overflow beyond the bounds of good sense—when it swallows a man up instead of providing him with the means to come to himself. No one who is not prepared to let the true spiritual and religious meaning of work, physical work included, act as a spur to keen good work on his own part, can claim to have a vocation to renounce outward possessions. He would merely lapse into indolence.

Equally opposed to the spirit of poverty is the desire to keep the tit-bits for oneself, taking it for granted that others can make do with the second-best. Possessive greed can attach itself to little things too, and a man will busy himself unceasingly in his immediate circle of interests, with things that may be worthless in themselves but where trespassers will be prosecuted. Naturally certain things are reserved for personal use; after all, each man's body is his own and no one else's. It is this non-interchangeability that distinguishes it from outward possessions. And the more closely things serve for protecting and tending the body, the more they share this incapacity to serve for common use, the degree varying according to social conditions and the level of civilization. But man's natural instinct is to extend this sphere disproportionately by anticipating all sorts of possible future needs and withdrawing a number of things from general use in case he should want them some time. The craving for security through ownership crops up again in connection with little things long after a man has ceased to need to worry about larger ones. But it is evident that the size and value of possessions are not the decisive factor when a man's freedom or lack of it are concerned, but his own behaviour. To administer a large property as a Christian, in a spirit of service to one's fellow men, is nearer to the mind of Christ than to be self-seeking in little things simply because the bigger ones are absent. Under those conditions the cares and troubles of administrating large properties are no obstacle but a positive means to being more and more Christian.

TRUE RICHES

An attitude of genuine Christian poverty throws open the doors to a world of higher values, it realizes ownership in the true sense without encountering the dangers inherent in property. True ownership guards a man in his freedom and erects a rampart around his individuality inside which he can find room to grow, relieved of too urgently pressing cares; and the time and energy saved can be dedicated to higher spiritual values. Safeguarded by property, his freedom is no longer threatened; he is no longer exposed to the possibility of being reduced to slavery by sheer brute force or deprived of his individuality by the withdrawal of things necessary to life.

Man achieves self-expression in practising his skill on things, growing, and growing-up, as he learns to manipulate them, and then he has something to show what he is capable of. However, the real product of all human creative work is not the object exhibited, though this aspect, too, is immensely important for the body-bound spirit of man—but it consists in a man becoming finer, better, more richly endowed, with a corresponding increase in the spiritual riches available to mankind as a whole. This is immediately evident in any activity beyond the mere satisfaction of everyday needs. Not the fees Rembrandt charged for his pictures endure and remain significant, but the opening up of a new aspect of life, an experience renewed from generation to generation, each in turn making the visible world richer than it was before.

The same is true of all art; it applies to the statesman who establishes order and provides better conditions of life; and to the scientist when his discoveries extend the scope of a freedom too narrowly confined by material needs, making room for the spirit to enter and find itself at home; or to the historian opening up new vistas of opportunities for man to seize, to the greater benefit of mankind in general. It can be realized by physical work too, making a man more of a man, for bodily activity is never alone in the field, leaving the spirit out of it. Focusing attention on the true durable effect of work and seeing to it that *this* aspect come to the fore for man to seek his satisfaction in— that is the function of poverty. The more spiritually-minded a man is, the less does he care for property as such, as history shows: with increasing clarity he sees it as the occasion and opportunity to devote himself to things of higher value. Thus wealth voluntarily renounced provides the best conditions for the realization of Christian poverty, for even great wealth, when linked to exalted motives, allows for a certain freedom: that liberality and magnanimity which Aristotle required of a noble-minded man, and which are in fact akin to true poverty.

Christian poverty does not despise human values and values proper to the world, not does it underestimate their importance. But it knows what a snare they can be—and the more refined they are the greater the danger—when they presume to set themselves up as absolute values. A man of some distinction is not easily taken in by the more sordid of life's attractions. If he is to lose himself, there is more likelihood that he will do it in art, scholarship or other branches of culture. Freedom must be safeguarded here too, but poverty has something else in mind, because these sorts of values are only accessible to the few—to any real extent. Most people hardly keep their heads above water, dealing with the cares and worries of earning a livelihood for themselves and their dependants, but it is precisely these people, the majority, that the example of poverty can fortify, pointing out where the permanent value of their work lies—work in itself so unassuming, so unlikely to attract attention, with so little to show for it afterwards. The highest virtue of work—to be found in conjunction with the smallest things precisely because it is the highest—a virtue accessible to man as man always and everywhere—is the endeavour to become unselfish and to love unselfishly. It is promised eternal life. It is a lot to ask that all work be done only in that spirit, but it is what Christian poverty requires, and is to be taken seriously all the time. A man will put a brake on his expenditure and turn his mind to examine the significance of the efforts he made to earn the where-withal, and immediately the economic yardstick ceases to be the only one.

It is an attitude that induces man to take things of higher value seriously again, to turn his gaze towards them and find his peace of mind in gearing his work accordingly. Thus voluntary poverty confers nobility, if we may use the term of one who does not live solely for his own sake and for the satisfaction of his appetites, but has an eye open for higher things. These have no necessary connection with property. The beauties of nature do not have to be owned to be enjoyed. In fact the owner is in constant danger that the cares of ownership will slip like dark clouds between him and natural beauty, concealing it from him. The higher a value is, the less the opportunities and fulfilment it offers have to do with actual external legal ownership. This is true from the elementary stage of discovery and recognition onwards. Economic values, being the nearest to matter in the human sphere, require an appropriate display of earthly means and are closely dependent on wealth. And political power and state power also require a great accumulation of material goods as their foundation. It is plain where the proper place for material goods is to be found: not at the top but at the bottom of the scale. Their function is the intermediary one of providing play-room for higher values. But if material things are at the bottom of the scale of values, they are nonetheless the ones that claim immediate attention, for life without nourishment is incapable of surviving even for a short time, so little strength can it draw out of itself.

The higher values are much less closely dependent on material things. Great works of art, great discoveries of a non-technical nature often come into existence under very trying conditions of life. We wonder whether these conditions were not actually the ones most likely to stimulate their production. And least of all is individual virtue bound to earthly means, being a putting into effect of personal values conducive to the expansion and abundant fulfilment of all other values. Here above all the decisive factors are the power of a man's heart, the integrity of his mind, and they are not frustrated by outside circumstances and ill-will. In giving up his life man may attain to himself and the highest virtue of all may be realized in death itself. Poverty, with the consequent restrictions and suffering, is no obstacle. Christian personality comes to fulfilment through love. Poverty frees a man from being entangled in his property and becoming a prey to anxieties, and it is thus conducive to selfless love.

By concentrating our minds on essentials, voluntary poverty does us all an inestimable service. The Poor Man of Assisi is a supreme example. Poverty discovers the real values of property and work, the values which truly make men rich and bring them happiness. It tells the property-holders what their property is there for; it reminds them of the inherent obligation of a Christian, making it impossible for a rich man to remain in unruffled enjoyment of his possessions, wrapped in affable self-satisfaction; poverty is often an inopportune and unwelcome danger-signal, even a hated one. Once justice is done to life's requirements, a man has a right to riches only in so far as he places them at the service of those higher values, the ones that make life richer for all, or for as many as possible. And love comes first, love that helps those in need and offers people—as many as possible—the means to extract themselves from their difficulties, setting up conditions in which a worth-while human life can be lived.

Love gives working people a sense of the real purport of their efforts. Physical work is heavy and oppressive. Done for its own sake it is a curse. Moreover in the economic conditions prevailing today it is largely monotonous and one-sided, in fact seen in isolation it is in itself senseless. And precisely this senselessness, using only one side of a man, and the least intrinsically human side too, has appalling after-effects. What is senseless leaves a man empty. Hence the bitterness which fills the hearts of so many working people; they feel they are cheated of what really constitutes life. True, they often seek it in the wrong place, they think if only they were rich they would have all their heart's desire. But their sense of rebellion is deeply justified: what they are really looking for is a human meaning for their work. This meaning can only be the Christian one of understanding work as development of personality, through love seen as service, love for the family that is housed and fed on the proceeds of the work; love for the community which is served by setting to work on a given job, one which has meaning only in relation to the whole: a whole made up of a combination of jobs which together compose its explicit function and produce what is expected of it.

The knowledge that work as such is never done in vain; that a man is never just a beast of burden being slowly worked to death, simply in order to leave his children to the same fate: this knowledge makes the daily lot bearable, keeping him on terms with himself and safe-guarding what is finest in him from suffering damage. The Christian worker sees further than his pay-packet. He knows what is essential and finds peace and happiness in it. The bitterness which oppresses him—himself first of all and most deeply—melts like the frozen earth in warm spring sunshine. If only both sides had the Christian concep-tion of property and work, how easily the conflicts between employers and employees would lose their bitterness. It would still be necessary to come to terms over the economics of work and the proper distribu-tion of profits, for changing conditions call for solutions at every stage. But the danger is no longer imminent that those who happened to be in power would take advantage of it to bully and exploit the others, or even, given the circumstances, reduce them to slavery under dictatorship. Without an inner spirit of Christian poverty neither class nor class-war will disappear nor the hatred and bitterness they engender. If the movement to liberate the workers from unworthy living conditions tends to bring them into still greater subjection, it is because man is so much involved in his senseless materialism that he sees work and property as merely economic questions, with force—

which is matter's only outlet—as the only means to achieve redress. A materialist cannot of course admit that the way to freedom is not through economic means but through spiritual powers which must therefore be given support. That is why there is so little freedom still, and why the world is in danger of falling a prey to the unscrupulous domination of a group of criminals. So Christian poverty as an endeavour to achieve inner freedom from the craving for property and economic power has a great social task before it. Only in the spirit of Christian poverty can property-holders understand the necessity of admitting the workers' right to conditions of life worthy of men: conditions under which they can live humanly, not as beasts of burden. And in the same spirit the workers themselves will discover the best methods for achieving this end.

Finally, the truth and the error of the heathen conception of God should now be clear: it still influences our ideas. God is prosperous, say the heathen. This is both true and false. False, if his prosperity is taken to consist in earthly possessions. God possesses nothing if property is supposed to consist in an exclusive right to things for one's own maintenance. God has no need of material goods for his existence, which issues purely from himself. But this does not mean that he excludes his creatures from the right to make use of what he created. In terms of ordinary prosperity, we may say: God is poor; he possesses nothing, he has nothing. He is poorer than a man can ever be, for no man can entirely do without material goods. But this poverty is only the reverse side of God's boundless prosperity; God *has* nothing because he *is* everything.

When God's great spiritual abundance elected to take human form, it was done in a state of almost complete destitution in regard to property. Christ achieved the superhuman work of redemption without the support of earthly wealth and political power, revealing how powerful the spirit in him was. It was the power of God himself. The poverty of Christ leaves no ground for supposing that his work, which has gone on living all down the centuries, was dependent on earthly means, on their size and abundance. Christ was property-less all his life till finally reduced to extremest destitution on the Cross, and this should make us aware of the nature of spiritual power and of the true riches that revive all who are weary and burdened. How unselfish all ownership would have to be in order to cease to do harm, is shown in Christ's attitude, incomprehensible as it may be to the natural view. The miraculous powers he had constantly at his disposal as Son of

God were never used to alleviate his own pain and make his own life more comfortable. They were there to be given away, to help others in need, and to reveal the glory of the kingdom. Whoever sees him in the act of giving sees his heavenly Father, who bestows his bounty on evildoers as well as on the good (Matt. 5. 44 ff.) and gives ungrudgingly. Through the glowing power of his loving heart Christ was able to give more in his own state of earthly poverty than any man could ever do, however rich. Giving, as his example shows, is above all a spiritual act, enriching the giver. Not in firmly held possessions, not in possessiveness, but in sharing, is true wealth to be found, and it is akin to divinity. Material goods diminish through distribution; the more there are to receive, the less each actually has. But spiritual goods are all the richer and fuller for being widely shared. Hence, 'It is more blessed to give than to receive' (Acts 20. 35).

If God has nothing because he is everything, then man's aim can also be, to *be* as much as possible; and with this personal power of being as his base, to work for good. Happiness is to be found in what one is. When a man is nothing and is oppressed by the sense of his own emptiness and worthlessness, he seeks vainly for consolation and peace, happiness and bliss, in property and power. Voluntary poverty is the attempt to live so strongly upon the inner surge of love for Christ and its radiance, that external supports can be reduced to a minimum, and this minimum no longer constitutes private property as such, the use of things being through dependence on another man's will, dependent on God alone, so that the power of the spirit can operate without let or hindrance. That divine power which maintains matter in existence must be taken into account again; as many people as possible should once more, with Christ, St. Francis of Assisi and so many other saints, grasp the world literally as the constant product of the outpouring of God's abundant mighty love.

A new awareness of the true nature of things grows out of the change of attitude which poverty effects in a man. It is natural to see things as there-for-me. Things seem to be compounds of potential usefulness and potential dangers—a surface-effect through which the thing-in-itself appears dimly as base and background. That bodily life with its cares imposes such a view of material reality is a fact that has often been explained by saying that the senses are only capable of apprehending appearances, behind which true being lies concealed. But in reality man's mind is just as responsible as his senses for this one-sided attitude to things. Every perception is a spiritual act but it is bound to the body and therefore possesses certain special sensory characteristics.[1]

Phenomenology is an attempt, confined to cognition, to exclude the utility-factor and apprehend the being of things in itself.[2] That is why it induces the philosopher to take up a new attitude to things.

It is immediately clear that this new attitude is akin to poverty. And the insistence of platonism on preparing for philosophical cognition by ascetic means is wholly comprehensible. Nevertheless, philosophy is purely concerned with cognition, and outside its own sphere it does not foster an attitude of disinterested objectivity. On the other hand poverty has no philosophical or scientific interests of its own. Its claim is not pure knowledge for its own sake, but man's improvement. However, we see why it is that in antiquity philosophers in particular paid attention to the value of poverty and frugality; and also how the philosophical attitude of disinterested perception, as well as the endeavour to attain to perfection, both tend to make a man incapable of discerning whether a thing is useful or harmful for his purposes. Hence the philosopher's proverbial ignorance of the world, and the saint's still more—and lack of skill in practical matters, from the point of view of those to whom knowledge of the world consists in a keen sense of where one's own advantage lies.

So the new outlook of poverty has a certain kinship with phenomenology. It is a religious outlook. It might appear just as one-sided in its way as the usual approach to things with the dominating concern for a livelihood. And in fact it has often been accused of neglecting the good things of the earth and concentrating only on the other world. That such a danger exists is not to be denied. But it does not lie in poverty as such but in a false understanding of its spirit, and more often still, in human insufficiency in putting it into practice.

Things are mutually exclusive in relation to one another; their relation to God, however, is in quite a different category. They are of God's making, each in its own particular nature is an effect of God's, displaying in reflection one feature of his immeasureable abundance. That is why the being of things is important for the religious outlook. The more closely it is contemplated, the better it reveals God. The more radiant it is, the more gloriously does the brightness of its Creator shine through. And indeed the saints themselves, as they approach perfection, attain to a new loving joy in nature and its

[1] Cf. A. Brunner's work on the graded structure of the world (*Der Stufenbau der Welt*, pp. 104 ff.).

[2] *Ibid.*, pp. 115 ff. A. Brunner: *La Personne Incarnée*, Paris, 1947.

splendours. In fact it was they who first opened men's eyes to the beauty of nature and the artists followed in their wake. All art has its origin in religion and its evolution always witnesses to changes in man's religious conception of the world. For the attitude of the artist is akin to the disinterested view of the saint. It is, like philosophical perception, a moment in his total attitude.

If a Christian's reaction at this stage is to shrink away from things with their disturbing beauty, that is only transitory. He is not, he feels, strong enough spiritually to look at them in pure love, making no demands, and therefore no more subject to temptation on their account. His urge to hold and enjoy is still too clamant for there to be no danger of egoism pouncing upon them and thus taking on a new lease of life. Until a man has passed through apparent death and that terrible negative stage of renunciation, he is incapable of entering into a right relationship with things and being what he is supposed to be—their friend, as part of the same creation and God's child. So long as he is only concerned with one side of things, and only from his egoistical angle, he has no interest in seeing them plain and simple as they are in the round. The more he considers their being exclusively as being-for-him, the more terribly does doing-without seem like watching them fade away in a world deprived of all reality. Until at last their true full being dawns on his new way of seeing. Even this has been distorted under the influence of philosophical theories, the possibility of this total apprehension of reality being misunderstood as a general perception of universality as such, in which particularities were supposed to disappear—that is to say, a much less complete perception, overlooking precisely the irreplaceable quality of each separate thing: which is that it is unique, existing once for all; a unique and irreplaceable representation of God.

Through this religious view of the world, the royal priesthood to which every Christian is called comes into its own (1 Peter 2. 9). By using them aright, man gives things an orientation towards their true destiny, and in a certain sense brings them back home to their Author. They can never enter into God in the full sense open to man, but when he has once been transfigured himself, he becomes their mediator and proxy for union with God. Thus Christian poverty is a true priesthood, raised to the highest degree in the sacraments, where the elements of matter become the signs and means of grace. Adherence to Christian poverty brings about that perfect transformation of things for which all creation groans (Rom. 8. 19 ff.). It is the poetic transformation in which Rilke sees the meaning of life,[1] only far far more profound, more lasting, more real. And it is accessible to all, not only to the specially gifted poet or the man endowed with worldly goods. That harrowing transitoriness of possessions is overcome. And the transformation lasts forever, for it is only in appearance that we are 'the most transient' and 'the most perishable'.

This priesthood is royal. For Christian poverty makes a man free and redeems him in himself from the compulsion of earthly goods. In royal independence he stands above them, his gaze raised to the All-Highest, and he makes use of them for his own ends unhindered. He alone possesses things in the true sense because he transforms them, takes their beauty in within him, and finds his way down through their being to the very ground of it. In grateful love to their Creator he comes to their very source—in faith meanwhile, till the day of seeing face to face has come. As they were for a St. Francis of Assisi, so they will be for him: all created things brothers and sisters here and now, no longer alien and obscure. God's creative goodness will shine through them more and more clearly, as before the Fall.

Not suffering and diminution are the true meaning of poverty, but rather exaltation and joy. It is more than a coincidence that the Poor Man of Assisi was a joyful saint, and that St. Luke's Gospel, the gospel of poverty and love of neighbours, is at the same time the gospel of joy and peace. Man all too easily believes that joy depends on outward conditions, and above all on as large an amount of earthly goods and luxuries as possible. Pleasure of the senses alone can produce no joy and therefore fails to satisfy for long. The chief source of individual, happy-making joy lies within a man, in his capacity for enjoyment and happiness. It is up to man to foster this capacity and keep it alive. With the growing force of his personal being comes increasing power to transform all things for joy. He finds outlets in ever greater abundance and his own heightened capacities open up new sources of joy. Assuredly even in this state a man is not wholly independent of external things, he is after all soul *and* body. But the more spiritual and free he has become, the more his centre of gravity shifts from the precarious world of things to the true centre of his being; and his joy, too, will depend correspondingly little on material considerations and conditions. Poverty teaches him to observe the beauty of small commonplace things, it opens his eyes to their splendour and to the incomparable glory of what lies close at hand. It is an attitude of mind which dis-

[1] *Duineser Elegien*, 9th Elegy.

covers in everything an occasion for praising God, as is so wonderfully expressed in the *Benedicite*; an attitude in which things are pointers to God's goodness, prompting to gratitude and trustfulness, and it is conducive to pure selfless joy in the beauty of created things—the inimitable beauty of what the hand of God has given.

As the child so confidently trusts in his parents, so does redeemed man discover in all things, renewed day by day, the watchful Fatherly love of God in which he may put his whole trust and fear no more. It is precisely through this joy, with all self-seeking eliminated, that Christian poverty is revealed as true riches, the only sort of wealth that satisfies a man entirely. He who lives on thanksgiving, joy and love is in truth a happy man.

Transfiguration of the world, return to the original state of innocence and detachment, that is the meaning of poverty. Certain people can bring it about to an astonishing degree—invisibly; and it will all become visible when once the Lord returns to restore all things. Meanwhile, here and there, the transfiguration breaks through in isolated instances in our own world of time. When a man has grown free from the will-to-possess, from egoistical acquisitiveness, then God's gifts can be entrusted to him without danger. It seems even as though these gifts gravitate to him, slipping into his hand, wanting him to make use of them. What mountains of money and earthly goods have been handed out and distributed by the saints of Caritas! How it all came pouring in when they needed it. But only as much as was needed at that moment. They were not to live in security. They were not to have enough for years ahead. They were to live trusting that God's help lay ready for the right moment but not sooner. They were to believe and know that God is never too late, for nothing can come without him.

Those gifts of the saints contained a wonderful healing power for souls. They were filled with calming, comforting benevolent strength. They were far more than merely assistance for the immediate needs of the body. They came as messengers of God's love like St. Elizabeth's roses; that is why such benediction lay upon them. Matter had become what it was before the Fall and should always have remained, the bearer and mediator of God's grace and power. In the wonderful occurrences we read of in the lives of certain saints, in the multiplying of supplies for helping the many, we see visibly what happens invisibly in every gift which is given in true love: we see the fact that every true gift is worth far more than its earthly value and the purely material help it can bring, and is for the soul too a gift and an enrichment. A gift is more than the mere transfer of a material object, for it is a human, that is to say, first and foremost a spiritual event.

It is thus that Christ transformed the material world through the power of his love. How well he loved the scenes and the scenery of his home country, immortalizing them in parables picturing the Father's loving-kindness! Where can we find anything to compare with the parables for veracity in rendering the earthly scene, and transparency in letting the spirit shine through unimpaired! The least events and happenings come forward as exalted symbols without for a moment losing their firm hold on everyday life. There is no sign here of dilution for pseudo-allegorical effects of dubious spiritual value. The way to the fields, the air, light, water, to bread and to home are all charged with mystery: the mystery of his human-divine life, the mystery of God himself shining through ordinary everyday things. The merest insignificant trifle becomes an incomparably apt and clear statement of the greatest and most ineffable truth. Christ saw the world as it is, and as it ought to be seen, as a radiance of his Father's love.

And he transformed it. What are the sacraments if not the beginning of the transfiguration which all creation awaits, full of expectancy (Rom. 8. 19 ff.)? Bread and wine, water and oil, so little in quantity and unassuming as they are, so important nonetheless for daily life, are signs and intermediaries of the highest graces, even of the grace of all graces, of the incarnate Son of God himself. It is precisely in the sacrament of the altar that the meaning of renunciation in poverty is clear, the apparent giving up of self for the sake of true being. How tiny the elements are of earth and matter, and the event is great beyond our comprehension, the blessing conferred rich beyond all telling; yet the elements are only enough to ensure that the symbol can be seen. But if bread and wine had human feelings, how they would bewail their loss of self in transubstantiation, stricken with terror till they perceived what great thing had befallen them, the greatest granted to any creature: to be transformed and taken in within the innermost heart of divine being. Bread and wine do not know what happens to them, they do not undergo any permanent change that they are aware of. But when we receive them in the sacrament we know what a great thing it is to be called upon to relax our hold on earthly goods in order to take part in that being which is the true eternal being of God, and to act and live from that hearth of new and inconceivable riches. 'Blessed are the poor in spirit, for theirs is the kingdom of heaven.'

CHAPTER THREE

Marriage and Chastity

THE FUNCTION OF MARRIAGE

FAR nearer to man's real self than property is sexuality, as near as the body itself. The body, to every man his own, is distinguished by the fact that it is not, like property, something external that can be separated from a man without endangering his life, but is nonetheless not to be identified with his true self. A man can still take an objective view of his body and its component parts, but he is at the same time implicated in them. There is such a close bond here in the physical sphere, and particularly in human sexuality such an interpenetration, that a person in search of perfection must take a definite stand in regard to it.

The human sexual instinct as such is there first and foremost to ensure the propagation of the race by the generation of a numerous healthy progeny. Thus far it is like animal sexuality. But here we have only a likeness, not identity. The difference lies on the human side in that closeness of the body to the personality of which we have already spoken; the spirit is the animating and quickening principle of bodily life.

Thus sexuality cannot be dismissed as largely irrelevant to human life as a whole, it is not merely a natural function. It always concerns a living person. That is why, where it is not used as a means of attaining to the greatest possible perfection, it is degrading. That is also why it was impossible for Christianity to disregard it. Christianity never condemned sex; on the contrary, through the raising of marriage to the dignity of a sacrament, it turned it into a means of sanctification. Neither did it underestimate the danger inherent in this powerful human instinct.

In Christian life as a whole, marriage has the main purpose of smoothing the way of growth into Christian perfection. Its natural function as the means of propagating the human race, far from being superseded, is included as an essential element of the main purpose. Marriage has thus become a high mystery (Eph. 5. 32): just as Christ gave himself up for his Church in selfless love, so shall man embrace his dearest in selfless love. Just as the Church depends on the one Christ and exists solely for his work, so shall a woman find her place close to her husband in true love and live for him and his concerns (Eph. 5. 22 ff.). The meaning of marriage is education in selflessness in a life-long relationship in which bodily intercourse paves the way for the spirit of mutual self-sacrifice and fosters it. Man and woman will no longer live each his own life, but live for one another and for their children. In animals, sexuality and maternal care for offspring is the first sign—a very imperfect and usually short-lived one—of the breaking-down of the isolation in which individual forms of life exist. Sexual relations are like a first indication of the nature of true love. And in the human sphere they are given this name of love, little though they deserve it when they are not more than mere sexuality.

In man, sex is willy-nilly penetrated with personality and whether he likes it or not he has to take it into account. This is what makes the sexual bond something more than merely physical as in animals. Of its very nature the relationship demands personal self-surrender in true love; otherwise the mere yielding of the body for self-satisfaction is personally degrading. If love is withheld, the act is impaired in the essence of its nature, not without evil effects for both parties concerned. In physical intercourse love is present and is love of a person. All life long the same person. So the marriage bond only ends with the death of one of the two partners.

The marriage bond is no purely spiritual one but necessarily includes the body too. That is why it is essentially exclusive in a way other relationships, e.g. friendship, do not need to be. Any number of people can come together in a bond of a non-physical nature without adversely affecting any one of them. But wherever matter and physical things are involved, this is no more possible. When a man eats a piece of bread, that is the end of the possibility that it will ever be eaten by other men. All property is essentially exclusive, as we saw earlier. What one man has is denied his neighbour. This is a law that holds good in marital relations too, in all that touches bodily intercourse, and much more stringently so than for property because a body cannot, like external goods, be replaced. Bodily surrender to a second person is an infringement of the total relationship already owed to the first, and is therefore forbidden. In marital love the close union of body with spirit makes it impossible for there to be more than one partner, and personal love will reserve sexual intercourse for this one partner for life.

The fact that the person as such is so inevitably and essentially involved is the reason for the very ancient and widespread custom of observing special religious rites before embarking on a marriage. This was intended and is intended to show that marriage goes far beyond the natural function on which it rests and reaches up into spiritual regions where the person as such counts. Moreover, here man has always more or less consciously felt himself to be in the presence of mysterious higher powers; as we know through Christianity, here he meets God himself. For as person he stands before God responsible, and all true and selfless love is accomplished in God's power. But in decadent times man is less and less aware of it and tends to treat marriage as a purely worldly matter. With the loss of that other attitude he lacks the strength to carry an unconditional bond through life and to take a stand once for all, as is incumbent on him as person; for only thus can the difficult situations of life and the obligations it entails be met and mastered creatively.

Inasmuch as a man, and a woman too, no longer think self-centredly, but as marriage partners they are there for one another and in course of time grow into one another spiritually, having all their interests in common, living from the one centre and source, they learn to rise to selfless love. Together they undertake the sacrifices involved in founding and bringing up a family and this is a training in true self-surrender for them both. The propagation of the race is, as we saw, not merely a physical process in marriage as it is in the animal world. Young people are not only born into life with bodies, they have to be trained to respond on the spiritual plane too, if they are to be truly human.

The authority of parents over children is distinguished from other forms of authority in that it is not based on rare gifts of personal insight into higher ways of life which are not immediately accessible to others; nor is it due to the practical requirements of work done in common, where direction is a sheer necessity—though both these forms of authority are elements in parental authority. But it arises chiefly out of the child's inability, for the time being, to make decisions for himself. His individuality is still too closely tied to sub-personal processes and can only gradually be set free by the educative influence of other people. So long as this state of helplessness lasts, the parents, as those who provided the child with life, the basis of all else, are in duty bound, as well as fully entitled, to take the child's place in regard to all matters affecting himself. They have to decide and act for him, as he would do for himself had he the capacity.

This acting on the child's behalf is no limited liability. It covers all that concerns the child as a person, it can only be perfectly done out of selfless love for the child, whose interests one identifies with one's own. To have a natural liking for children is a great help and makes this loving service on their behalf much easier to perform; but it is no guarantee of it. What is involved is a constant brake on one's naturally selfish instincts, always ready to reduce the child to a means of self-indulgence, concentrating on winning the child's affection rather than on giving him unbounded love.

More than any other natural authority parental authority resembles God's and is the agent of God's. Creation, preservation and redemption concern a person immediately and not merely indirectly; that is why God is so often addressed as Father. And because the parents have so specially and completely to represent the child in all respects, a function which falls to them by the very nature of things, there are parental rights which cannot be swept away or brushed aside by any other rights.

All other forms of authority are confined to special fields and only indirectly affect individuals as such. They are, therefore, metaphysically seen, below parental authority; and claims made on the child by other authorities have to be addressed to the parents so long as the child is incapable of making independent decisions. No one can take from the parents the right to bring up their own children, no one can free them from the duty to do so, except in exceptional cases where the parents are wholly incapable of it.

In its representational character, parental authority has the duty to rear the child for independence, to initiate him into the obligations of life, and thus in due course to make itself superfluous. This distinguishes it from God's authority which never comes to an end. To the degree that the child's capacity to make reasonable and free decisions awakens and grows, parental authority must withdraw and gradually turn into a loving way of giving counsel. This is often not easy for parents, particularly not when they have grounds for anxiety. But if parents fail at the right moment to relinquish their hold and continue to treat their grown children as in their early years, they do them very serious harm. Either they provoke bitter resistance to an abuse dimly felt to be unjust, a resentment which easily hardens into a permanent state of furious opposition to all authority, which is why St. Paul uttered his warning: 'You who are fathers, do not rouse your children to resentment' (Eph. 6. 4). Or on the other hand the children never really attain to the independence they need in order to be able to cope with life; all their life long inferiority complexes will encumber them: a most oppressive burden. Inspired by unselfish love, parents must run the risk of gradually leaving their children to be responsible for themselves.

In man and woman two separate lives meet, two ways of looking at reality and appraising it that are deeply divergent. The world of each is differently coloured and has a different taste. Man is naturally inclined to declare his point of view right and the other person's wrong. But in actual fact both are imperfect and, in many cases, subjectively coloured, partial views of reality. Differences of this kind are only special and particular instances of the general rule that all human understanding has to form its views from a body-base. Sex, heredity, age and environment, education and personal gifts, all affect our approach to reality. What is easily accessible for one remains more or less out of reach for another. This gives man's whole conception of the world a strongly individual tinge. Now this is a limitation that can sometimes be dealt with. In given instances it is possible to adopt various points of view in turn in order to complete the picture. But the more closely and directly the body is concerned, the less one can do about it. Sex-conditioned colouring of human understanding and appraisals of reality are quite immune to treatment of the sort described.

If man were merely a higher animal, as so many theories expressly or implicitly infer, a bundle of nature-bound psychic forces, he could never hope to escape from these straits. Nor would he even be aware of the conditions confining his mind. The animal has no idea that its world is only a biologically determined section of the whole of reality and that other sorts of animals see the same reality in a different way. There is nothing in its nature to make it want to climb beyond the limits of the species, outgrowing its specific existence and pressing on to the essence of a reality independent of itself.

But man is different. True, his body lays conditions on him which he cannot throw off at will. He cannot stop being a man and seeing the world as man, and a woman cannot stop being a woman. But what distinguishes them from the animal is this. As intelligent beings both are capable of communication and understanding. But the one who communicates throws open the door into his own world, while the one who understands can enter in and catch a glimpse of reality as seen through the eyes of the other, and his (or her) mind will be all the richer for the experience. Indeed it is precisely this sharing in someone else's mind that makes man really human, able to break out of the narrow straits of the individual viewpoint and at least draw nearer to his aim of attaining to a complete and purely objective view of reality, even if it is never reached. And it is only by an understanding attitude to unfamiliar communications that the two sexes' different approach to the world can be resolved. But communication and understanding are not simply natural factors, it is rather the person as such that has the freedom and the will to open out and approach another with understanding. How many marriages suffer from the inability to take the other person's point of view seriously! But only by dint of being taken seriously is the other receiving due acknowledgement.

Hence one of the main duties of marriage—and mutual attraction should produce an atmosphere congenial to a communion of opinions and views and to mutual concessions as well. It may all seem foreign to nature and remote from experience, but the will to achieve loving understanding can accomplish it. Man and wife will both admit that one person's point of view has no exclusive claims on truth, that it is one-sided and ripe for supplementation and readjustment. They will both work away steadily at establishing a community of views and the effect will make them capable of more objectivity and more breadth of humanity. Mutual comprehension has its bounds, of course, and here patience has to be acquired if what is incomprehensible is not to be rejected as sheer nonsense. Such a marriage of minds provides conditions for true love to thrive in, in the form of due acknowledgement of the marriage partner's individuality and personality; and in an atmosphere of love mutual understanding will prosper.

If a person succeeds in breaking down his own narrow standpoint in these circumstances, which are particularly exacting ones—though greatly helped by the presence of mutual attraction—the mind becomes capable of surmounting the narrowly individualistic point of view in relation to other people too. It is hardly necessary to point out how important such readiness of understanding is in life with one's fellows. Man is by nature enclosed in his own opinions as though spellbound in them, a prisoner of his own views. Whatever does not agree with them is of course error or falsehood. But how can this be productive of anything but friction and dislike? Coming together is only possible when a person discovers how to break down the barriers egoism has set up and tried to look at things from another's standpoint, doing justice where justice is due. In fact it simply means acknowledging the other as a person. Being truly human depends in the last resort on the degree to which one can bring oneself to do this.

Such an intention of mutual understanding is not content with merely acknowledging the other person. Personality is many-sided and exchanges take place all along the line. Angles become less sharp, deficiencies are countered through the loving intercourse of marriage. Not that the man will be less manly, the woman less womanly. On the contrary, mutual compensation will stress and enhance the individuality of each. The man's strength grows more chivalrous and gentle through unselfishness; and the woman's natural tenderness becomes filled with a quiet glow of strength.

A marriage conducted along such lines as these means that man and woman in maturing acquire great goodness and kindness. The point of gravity in life together gradually shifts right over into a community of spirit with a deep inner sense of belonging to one another for a lifetime in common, a life freely accepted, come what may. All that is of the body becomes increasingly the expression of a deep spiritual union. And less and less is the body an obstacle to the transparency which belongs to love and life together, a transparency inherent in the spiritual togetherness of two people in love. The resulting attitude of unselfish caring for others will be of benefit beyond the bounds of the family circle. A man who is truly good is good to all, even though he cannot render assistance to all equally, but devotes his energies first to those who are his special charge, and only afterwards finds ways of helping other people. Kindness makes man like God, it fits him to be taken up into God's life.

THE DEMANDS OF NATURE

This ideal conception of marriage is seriously contaminated because of the Fall. The sexual instinct does indeed represent a first opening out and breaking through of self-contained individual being; but if we take genuine unselfishness on the personal level as our criterion, where its own function is concerned sex shows the most ruthless egoism. It has two possible modes of expression, dependent on whether it centres on the broader or the narrower ego. The natural function of the sexual instinct is to maintain the species. Among plants and animals individual life is sacrificed to this end, and its accomplishment is the highest function of their existence. And in man the sexual instinct takes the same direction. It too would use the individual as a mere means to perpetuate the species; being primarily physical, it is blind to any values higher than the propagation of as numerous and healthy a progeny as possible. But this brings it into conflict with the personal side of human life, which may never be turned into a means and a tool, for it is essentially being-in-itself. The common bond between personal being and bodily life and their inter-penetration give rise to a double-edged temptation at this point. Either the individual locks himself up in the egoism natural to the species; then he will live only for the extended ego of his group and place his own spirituality wholly at its service; or else he withholds sexuality from its natural function: not for the sake of becoming his true self, however, but rather abusing the right of disposal which as a person he is entitled to exercise over sexual as well as other matters—seeking pleasure without admitting responsibility, though the two are intimately connected here.

The latter danger is a specially grave one, because of the particular nature of the bond between spirit and body in human life which we have already considered. As the soul is the spirit's animating and forming principle to build up the body and sustain it, life is radically bound to the spirit and the spirit to it. As a primary instinct of life, more than any other tending to engross the whole personality, sexuality is inseparable from personality. Any attempt to separate them is immoral. The attempt to enjoy sexual pleasure as though it had nothing to do with personality and was utterly indifferent to it is immoral. There is no sexuality in man that is devoid of spirit or can rid itself of spirit, and what is more, sexuality invades the spiritual sphere too. It springs from the bottommost depths of life where the spirit gives soul to matter, animating it and making it human. Prior to consciousness spirit and life are so interlinked that man is *one* in being, he does not think and act like a spirit that is merely lodged in a body. On this account sex in man is not simply ruled by life, as in animals. Down to his deepest nature he is impregnated with spirit and can only be kept on the right course by the action of the spirit. Human nature has no sharply defined limitations like animal nature, and man is not allowed to give free rein to his instincts in the name of so-called nature, for no such nature exists in his case. Man has the choice either of controlling his sex, working at it from within to turn it more and more towards its ultimate destiny, which is to bring about the inner freedom of individual being, through love. Or else of being dominated by sex in his very spirit, reduced to slavery and a prey to its exorbitant demands; for the spiritual affiliations of sex cause it to work to his own destruction.

Freud's libido theory was partly right. Sex is not the only instinct, but it is the deepest and strongest. None other drenches human life to such an extent. And it sets to work from depths to which consciousness has no direct access. But owing to his materialistic point of view, Freud laid one-sided emphasis upon the fact that sexuality is tinged with spirituality and can deeply influence it. And he stated his theory with such finality that it is apparently taken for granted that spirit is merely an effect, an expression of sex in disguise. He overlooked the fact that sexuality is intrinsically, and to a much greater degree, affected by the spirit. It is therefore inadmissible to explain spirit in terms of sexuality, just as it would be incorrect to see sex as merely a function of the spirit. What we have here, as in any other department of human life, is that two-in-oneness characteristic of the human body. Man is essentially one and yet cannot achieve perfect unity within himself. The body is animated by the soul, but not in such a way that the centre of gravity naturally reposes in the spirit, in which case life would be entirely conducted by the spirit and be amenable to it without stress and strain. Life confronts the spirit with a gravitational force of its own, though it could have no such thing but for the spirit. The characteristic nature of sexual temptation arises from this condition, as we shall see.

On the other hand, there would be no two-in-oneness if the spirit exhausted its resources in the act of animating the body, like the principle of an animal's life. Then there would be no super-consciousness—Freud totally overlooked this fact—and hence no possibility whatever of a life of the mind, of thought, speech, will; the super-consciousness alone has the capacity to exercise censorship—not the sub-conscious, as Freud supposed. This super-consciousness, in which the purest forms of human spirituality are to be found, is however not to be apprehended except together with the senses. It always appears as a sort of overflow, a heightening of sense-perceptions. From this super-consciousness issue life's properly spiritual impulses, controls and states. But they reach full human efficacy only by penetrating into the body, for our body-bound spirit can only move freely and deeply in company with the body.[1]

Spirit and sex are not separate contiguous functions but are bound together in human life, though with the spirit radiating out beyond it; only on this account is Freud's so-called sublimation possible at all. If the spirit were only the product of a purely natural libido, it is not

[1] A. Brunner, *Der Stufenbau der Welt*, Chaps. 2 and 4.

clear why it should not be in the same state of subjection as in animals. Nor is it comprehensible why this libido should be ashamed of itself— another feature unknown to animals. In actual fact shame springs from the experience of subjugation and overpowering humiliation with which the force of sex threatens human personality. In his super-consciousness, even when he is corrupt, man knows that the spirit is not intended to serve the senses, but on the contrary the latter should remain subject to the spirit. Sublimation itself is not to be thought of as a sort of displacement of sexual forces, as though these were the only ones that existed in man, constituting a reserve to draw upon either for sexual purposes or for higher activities, so that what is used in one way is no longer available for any other. That is much too mechanical a way of looking at it, and it is not even fair to the living body. The theory merely provides grounds for lewd prying into human concerns in order to detect signs of hidden sexuality here, there and everywhere. That such disguised sensuality exists at all is due to the special relationship of spirit and body.

However, very intrinsic transformations of sexuality are possible, through the strengthening of man's spirituality to a pitch bringing him much nearer to that perfect self-possession that was his portion before original sin. Such intensification of spirituality would also draw up into itself the life forces that belong to the depths of human nature. In man, sexual cravings are not held in check by instinct as in animals and directed solely to the propagation of the species. The freedom and self-possession of the spirit, with the soul as animating principle of life, result in a relaxation of the rigid bounds set by instinct. It is now left to man's freedom to keep his appetites within bounds. If the spirit still had its own place in the order of things, a place proper to it because of its God-ward bent, as before the Fall, this order would prevail as a matter of course in all that affects the soul. Sexual cravings would immediately have been directed towards man's ultimate welfare, and would thus be in place in the proper ordering of the whole of life. No express effort of will would be necessary, and still less any subsequent repression and overcoming of lust.

But now that the spirit is at variance with reality and has thus fallen into disorder itself, the soul too is distraught. The possibility of alignment towards the true welfare of the person was destroyed at the source, and the weakening of the spirit has resulted in the psyche having a very much looser hold on freedom, for it now goes its own way, regardless even of a man's express will. The disturbance is actually, metaphysically seen, anterior to the will. The impulses of nature and the impulses of the spirit are at war with one another (Gal. 5. 17) and in its frailty the spirit often has to admit defeat. Concupiscence is thus a result of original sin, but is not yet sinful in itself; it only becomes sin when it is freely consented to.[1]

Since the Fall, man has to see to it that with the help of grace spiritual order is restored in him. Thus the cravings of the body will gradually be appeased and come under control. But it is not to be expected that in this lifetime—apart from quite exceptional gifts of grace—disorders can be dealt with before they arise. Turning his mind to higher things, man must conquer those lusts that arise against his will even, and he must reduce them to right proportions by self-denial. But as spirit and soul are not two separate principles but one and the same, there still remains that deep-seated pressure of spirit on bodily life, and not only the contrary one of body on spirit. Such are the conditions of our life.

Now one fact is clear: how it decisively depends on a man's inner attitude which aspects of reality he is aware of in spontaneous observation, and which on the contrary remain unremarked. Everything depends on this attitude: one man will find almost anything to be sexually disturbing, while another, though no less strongly sexed, is seldom perturbed—it would be misleading to talk of repression in the latter case: nothing has occurred that could require repressing. Repression takes place when temptation is not overcome inwardly for the sake of something higher, but is only denied satisfaction for outward considerations. It is uninhibited living-to-the-full that leads to repressions; for questions of health, and social considerations, soon set a limit to sexual gratification, though the undisciplined instinct remains inwardly savage and unsatisfied. The spirit can impose a limit for the sake of higher things only by injecting it with spirituality and thus transforming it. Experience teaches in fact that a strong love between man and woman, when it is spiritually determined, allays sexual desire without dulling it. Only thus can the fact be explained how under the influence of Christianity relations between the sexes have gained in depth and richness. The appeasement of sex through its inclusion in the total ordering of life under the spirit's guidance constitutes a release from the demon of sexuality. It is an obligation laid upon marriage, as much as upon an authentically chaste life, to accomplish this release through an inward acceptance of purity, which shows

[1] Council of Trent, 5th Session.

itself in a sincere and candid ease of manner in relations with people of the opposite sex.

But instead of finding the right place for sex in life as a whole, the spirit may allow itself to be swallowed up by sex, with far more deadly results than in the case of other instincts. The peculiar thing about sexual temptation is its fascination. The tempting element in every temptation consists in the attraction of some sub-personal portion of man to something that makes a direct appeal to it. But man exists as a whole and the instinct or urge concerned can only work itself out by gaining the voluntary assent of the self-determining part of him. It is by nature blind to higher things and presses its claims even when to yield is injurious to man's wholeness. In every temptation therefore man is fighting not against an outside alien foe: this would not be so hard. No, but he is in conflict with himself, therein lies the danger in every temptation. Drawn downward by a force that belongs to his own being, man must still rely on himself to remain steadfast. In every temptation the self-hood of man is put into question and has to reassert itself.

But the nearer the temptation comes to the centre of personality, the more deadly is the danger, for that moment of being foreign and different from oneself, which is all a part of it, is correspondingly shorter. To assert his independence as a free agent he is forced to make a stand within an ever-narrowing circle and it is from this very much impaired foothold that he has to put up his defence. Where external attractions are concerned, the average man is keenly aware of that moment of 'feeling different'. Only when greed and avarice have become dominant passions, and when money is distorted into a symbol for all that life has to offer, it vanishes almost completely. Similarly the need for food lies more on the outside verge of life. A man may fairly easily succumb to the attractions of food and drink, seeing that it is his own life, himself in fact, that experiences the desire for food: complete self-control is not easy even here. On the other hand it seldom develops into a regular vice. Addiction to drink has other grounds of a psychic nature beyond the mere quenching of thirst: no one is immoderate in drinking water. What is sought in drink is intoxication, in order to forget about oneself. When a man's spiritual freedom is inadequate to deal with the cares and worries of life, they can thus be brushed aside for a while through a lowering of consciousness; or perhaps in a momentary feeling of physical uplift a man will seek a sort of pseudo self-hood, because he despairs of ever being able to reach to genuine self-hood.

From all this it is clear that the temptation to misuse sex is particularly sinister and dangerous. Apart from pride and hatred, which have their roots in individual being, no seduction comes so near to the personal centre of being. Moreover man is driven back upon his naked spirit to withstand a tug that has the whole weight of life behind it. Man as a unit, made up of body and soul, can win only if his body is a willing partner of the spirit's. But this is hardly ever the case. In his feelings man is on the side of sex, for in his consciousness the drive of life presses ahead of the spiritual urge and pushes it aside. Thus at the moment of temptation a man finds himself apparently powerless against his sexual instinct, as though all resistance were foredoomed to failure. Hence more than in any other case the ego is up against itself: a free, personal but evidently powerless ego faces a sub-personal, unfree ego charged with life. A man's own feeling is that he is shackled and bewitched. The seduction is all the more alluring in that here, unlike most other forms of temptation, no positive consent is demanded of him. Sex only requires that he let himself go; and thus gliding on and being drawn along, he feels for a moment that he is relieved of all responsibility, for an impersonal but active and compulsive force is in full control. Willy-nilly the ego lets itself be devoured. That is what is both sinister and captivating, even demonic, about sexual temptation. It invites man to place his self-knowledge and all the awareness that he possesses as a personal being at the service of a pleasant sensation, and to enjoy it exhaustively without being burdened with any sense of responsibility, as though one were not a person at all. The untroubled instinct-driven life of an animal, where responsibility is not in question, is not a source of pleasure to the animal for it has no means of distancing itself from its own life, nothing in it being capable of rising above it. So that is what man is out to enjoy: a pleasure based on the fact of being a person, yet coupled with an evasion of that sense of responsibility intrinsic to personality.

Seeing how sinister and dangerous sexual temptation can be, the common attitude to it is quite comprehensible: morality consists in withstanding it, and immorality in giving way to it. It is in his attitude to sex that man decides for or against his self-being, at the very point where it is most frequently and most precariously open to attack. It is not that sexual sin is of its nature the worst sin[1] but that the temptation

[1] St. Thomas, *S.Th.*, 1a, 2ae, Q. 73, a. 5.

is the most seductive, so that in ordinary speech seduction means seduction to this sort of sin. Since the natural point of gravity of his being subsided through sin into bodily life, man has always been entangled in sexuality. Its springs so deep down in life give it an uncanny force and its closeness to personal being an insatiability both awe-inspiring and horrifying. It is hardly surprising that it was taken for something divine (*vide* the history of religions). Fascinating and baleful at one and the same time is the experience that body and senses find in it, confusedly suggestive of a divine provenance and the possibility of merging into it. And it is equally comprehensible that sexuality has almost everywhere been seen as something sinister and evil that defiles a man and makes him impure. Thus in heathendom sexual debauchery belonged to the service of the gods and so did sexual restraint and purity, the latter however was as a rule only external. But real defilement lies not in the sexual act as such but in the entanglement of the person and his freedom when the urge becomes obtrusive. This however is merely the reverse side of the weakness of individual self-hood, a result of apostasy from God (cf. Rom. 1. 24 ff.). That is why shame is the natural means of veiling off the whole field. It is a means of making apparent how precarious the condition of personal freedom and independence is, when exposed to the enticements of sex and to the force of sex. It arises from a dim awareness that to yield to this power, when it is not done in the service of true love for a person, is a sideslip and a swallowing up of a person's own self and thus signifies a deep wound to human dignity. The spirit is ashamed of its own powerlessness.

All this shows how it is not only the forbidden satisfaction of this instinct that is incompatible with the dignity of man as person, but that even permissible sexual activity in marriage always involves the danger that a person will be too much overwhelmed by the sheer force of the urge and give way to indulgence more than is justified. Such a marriage fails to perfectly fulfil its purpose, which is a training in selflessness and liberation from self-love in order to serve. The danger of reducing the marriage-partner to a mere tool, degrading to both parties, is always imminent. It poisons marital relations at the root and it is hardly surprising when the whole of life in common is wrecked and incessant bickering is the outcome, in the place of quiet loving accord.

If people do not get rid of egoism, they cannot be happy in marriage. When the man demands that his wife should be there for him alone and devote herself entirely to making life agreeable for him, and when a woman makes the same claim on her husband, then two egoisms clash and neither will give way, each doing great harm to the personal dignity of the other. No one dare seek the whole wherefore and why of his existence in another person. To claim so much is debasing and shocking even when done in apparent love. Genuine love loves to give but makes no claims on its own behalf; any claims it makes are for the good of the beloved. Their physical closeness to one another and their intimacy are bound to produce a situation where daily and hourly rubs occur, when true reverence for the personal dignity of the other partner has already been infringed. But each takes his own egoism as a matter of course so long as he has not managed to extract himself from it, and thus he will never see anything but the egoism of his partner, and will rise up in wrath to defend himself against it as an attack on his own rights, putting the whole blame for the constant quarrels on the other partner.

When a man or a woman gives way to egoism in such a dominant thing as sexuality, it becomes a destructive factor in human relationships.

With varying degrees of coarseness or subtlety, both sexes are liable to treat the selfhood of the partner with disparagement; and thus on the natural plane the relations of the sexes to one another are a mixture of attraction and conflict, they can neither live together nor apart. The stronger the physical attraction is, the more dogged the struggle for mastery will be. Only an equally sustained and earnest effort in the direction of genuine unselfish love can gradually heal the resultant discord. The body is necessary to their love as intermediary. There is no understanding between people and no intercourse of minds and souls without speech and communication. But the intermediary of the body alone makes it possible for two people to bring the very core of the spiritual life of each into contact with the other and to appreciate one another and live for one another wholly. The intense and in intention perfect living for one another by 'becoming one flesh' (Matt. 19. 4–6) is the purpose of marriage; it is thus that it is fulfilled and perfected.

But the body is not only this admirable medium for good. We saw how discord arises over cultural matters, and it reappears in this sphere, greatly enhanced. Cultural things are of physical provenance after all, and the body is both medium and obstacle too. Bodily life possesses the properties of matter intrinsically, and that self-contained quality of matter is apparent here and can never entirely be got rid of by natural human energies alone. Thus that ultimate transparency for one another which is so essential a part of perfect love can never be realized, just as man is never wholly transparent to himself. Two people remain strangers to one another to the degree that each is a stranger to himself. Love comes up against this dark patch in others as though it were a wall which, solid though it be, is not to be allowed to hold them up. Then the temptation is great, instead of letting be in all loving patience, to forge ahead and force the issue: using means to win through to perfect union which are simply destructive of love; or seeking it not above but below, in intoxication, loss of self-control, loss of self. All this only makes a man more of a stranger to himself; he shifts his focus to the fringe of those sub-personal regions where freedom is no more in control but only instinct. Then disappointed love easily turns to hate, striving to bring about that impossible total appropriation of the beloved one by destructive means.

A similar distortion through egoism threatens the relations of parents to children. There is always the danger that they will not actually love the children but themselves in them: they enjoy the delightful feeling of being tenderly loved by them. The child is no longer here in his own right, and there is not enough room made for him. As a result he does not get the direction he needs: a guidance full of loving insight and thus dependable. He is either coddled and spoilt or made inwardly insecure by desultory treatment as the mood dictates. And naturally the child will suffer great harm to his soul if the love of his parents is lacking and he feels he is a burden to them. In all these respects parents may betray the high charge which is laid upon them to educate their child till he reaches honourable and responsible manhood, and to grow better themselves in the course of doing it.

The natural function of the sexual instinct is the maintenance of the species. Even on this level man lays traps for himself and with the best will in the world may still trip up. Man's ego has no spatial delineation, it extends beyond the body to include his possessions, and still more, family and relations. His most painful experiences touch his possessions and his body. Hence the strong natural tendency to rope the family into the sphere of the ego. Actually what happens is, as we saw, an initial breaking down of that self-containment of the individual which should be linked to the opening up of the self through love, and should facilitate this. But being personal, this opening-up through love reaches far ahead of instinct, and the capacity of sex to rise above itself is weak and limited; but sex is inevitably involved and is now borne along into a sphere in which it has no further direct function at all, and it strenuously resists being dragged up out of its own field. Instinct would prefer settling down in the small circle of family and friends, kith and kin, and living for these alone. So there arises a new form of egoism, an expanded but nonetheless dangerous one: married egoism and family egoism.

That a man feels impelled to care for his own and make great sacrifices for them is still an effect of the natural aspect of sexuality. But there is also the danger that instead of living in the narrower ego a man will now live for the extended ego of family and relations, making no real effort to overcome his egoism at all. The circumference of the ego is extended to include kindred, class, club, nation and state: all will be regarded and defended with the same party-prejudice. At this stage a man's whole concern is for the well-being and advancement of that smaller or greater circle of his. Like the individual ego, this enlarged ego now occupies the centre of the world and is the sole touchstone for everything.

Group interests will be pushed forward as a matter of course, regardless of the rights of others. We see this tendency to treat kindred and family as absolute in the history of religions, in the forms of ancestor-worship and deification of the state. Ancestor-worship has a sound basis, just as care for the family has. Every man owes a debt of gratitude to his parents and through them to his forebears. But over and beyond this, ancestors have often been turned into a divine power with which the fortune and well-being of the tribe is supposed to have a natural connection. This has led to the subjugation of the individual to the tribe, for to be separated from it, whether by right or not, placed a man outside the range of the only form of welfare available to him. In the last resort, deification of ancestors represents a granting of absolute and ultimate rights to the vital principle.

The temptation to which enlarged egoism is exposed is all the more dangerous for not blatantly coming forward as such and being dismissed as such, as with individual egoism. On the contrary, it appears as praiseworthy unselfishness; for man is capable of forgetting himself and making all sorts of sacrifices on its behalf, never observing that in the expanded circle of his ego—in the position, influence and power of his family, his class or his nation, he is merely seeking security and acknowledgement for himself; just as any misfortune that befalls it affects him as though it had happened to his own body. Certainly the performance of services on behalf of the family is more worth while than ordinary selfishness, just as in biology the species takes precedence of individual forms of life. Nonetheless it is not far removed from a merely natural function and is a check on a man's freedom so long as he does not transform it by means of what is intrinsically human in him.

How comprehensible it is that in the course of history endeavours to achieve social justice so often come up against the family and seek to wreck it. Even Plato considered it necessary to deny family life to the ruling class in order to avoid abuses of power. It is in fact usually the family or the tribe or clan that is the holder of wealth and therefore of political power. Tribal egoism as described can easily produce a situation in which power is manipulated almost entirely to its own advantage. Nonetheless all efforts to set the family aside are a ghastly mistake, not at all conducive to achieving the aims of social justice. For it is not the family and the tribe that are the source of injustice, but man's natural egoism. If this egoism is officially sanctioned, if it is positively encouraged by inciting people to hatred and violence, the abuse will not cease, but simply take on other forms. That is what made Christianity turn to other means, as we shall see, when it was a matter of breaking tribal predominance and securing for the individual the freedom that is his due.

And it would be absurd to say that preoccupation with family or group interests is merely the outlet for a natural instinct and nothing more. That is not true. As in all things human, here too we have the double pull of nature and spiritual personality. It is simply a matter of breaking down the narrower view and laying bare the prejudices. Then at last justice becomes possible, and then, too, proper concern for the well-being of family, class and country can be a starting-point towards genuine true love, and a means to attain to it.

It would be wrong to try to achieve this purpose by doing away with all ties of family, status and nationality. Without ties a man becomes a rolling stone and loses touch with reality. He mistakes reality for a wholly spiritual thing and as a consequence his activities tend to be destructive rather than constructive. The mind is powerless to work and influence the world without the body. But in admitting this, man has to accept all the bonds and limitations proper to his nature. It is through spiritual transformation that the expansion of what is purely natural occurs, till it surpasses itself. Without such transformation true human values cannot come to light.

It is an endeavour where the real mean between the two extremes is never immediately apparent but has to be discovered and re-discovered. A man succumbs more easily to the temptation to lose himself in the distances of non-reality, and over and beyond his profession to neglect his married life and family; a woman on the other hand may tend to want to shut herself up with her husband in the small circle of home and family and regard all other claims as unwelcome intrusions. It is significant that in his earthly life Christ committed himself to the narrow circle of his own home and country, as the encounter with the Canaanite woman shows (Matt. 15. 24). Here, as in all else, he remained truly man. But through the warmth and power of his self-surrender he transformed this bond, with its clear-cut system of obligations, into a vessel for the salvation of the whole world.

BETROTHED TO CHRIST

So we see how easily egoism slips in at every crack and cranny in marriage and family life. They are meant as an opportunity to practise unselfishness, and even sensual desires are challenged to show themselves generous; but all too often, in different disguises, more or less subtly, more or less brutally, self-love will be lord and master and will exploit the situation for its own purposes. Spirit ought to raise the body to be more and more the willing instrument of its striving towards goodness and freedom and its ally too. But the inner bond of spirit and body is a trap for the spirit, prompt with the temptation to it to abuse its status as seat of selfhood and become a tool of lust. Very deep down in human nature is that danger-spot where spirit and the stuff of the human body effect their union.

Christian chastity is intended as a means of restoring to human relationships the purity and unselfishness that are theirs by right. It is not to be accounted for by a wholesale condemnation of sex. As a judgement on marriage it is not to be thought of. The fact that celibacy spares a man a load of troubles and worries is also wholly irrelevant. On the contrary, love, true to its nature, impels a man to take other people's troubles and worries upon his own shoulders. No, to tot up the advantages of celibacy is a selfish and heathen act, not at all conducive to making chastity stand out in its true colours.

The real ground for Christian chastity is something totally different. It aims at the same thing as marriage ultimately and intrinsically does: self-surrender in the service of other people; but without the sexual bond and its attendant dangers. Just as poverty concentrates on that essential quality of earthly goods that does man good, and avoids exposure to the entanglements of property, so chastity seeks to realize the intrinsic part of marriage, the personal spiritual values, in renunciation of sex with all its allurements and inherent egoism. Far from rejecting true love of people, chastity does all it can to find suitable scope for it. It is aware that everywhere, and chiefly in marriage, it is the mind, the spiritually personal element, not the physical element, that animates and promotes human relations. Therefore chastity wishes to live the life of the spirit exclusively: at its best, a religious life. The chaste heart should never be empty of love but let love fill it to overflowing. All the high and noble aspirations of marriage, all the tenderness and intimacy that thrive in its enclosed garden, are not to be lost in chastity.

But the question faces us: whether all this is possible, and how. Such intimacy only arises naturally between people of opposite sexes and then it includes that impulsion towards the surrender of body and soul that has in marriage its appropriate conclusion. One might well wonder whether the love of God could replace it. Can a man and dare a man love God in that way? God who is most exalted purest Spirit? He is too far from our human understanding. We can have no idea of his inner life, for it is God's most holy mystery. God's life, his thoughts and feelings, so to say, are utterly beyond our range. As concrete and real, man only knows a life of human feelings and emotions, and here he is challenged to respond on that plane too. The heathen world seldom dared even to consider the possibility of such personal trust in divinity. It knew all about the essential distance between divinity and mankind. Only in two cases did it attempt union with God. Either the divine was submerged in the impersonal; and the more it was so, the more the purpose of life was seen in being thus absorbed by the impersonal. Resulting in utter loss of personality instead of its perfection, and a fall into non-being. Or on the other hand when man drew near to divinity through conceiving it as the almighty power ruling the life of the world, the relations of gods to the sons of men deteriorated to all-too-human a level, with sex paramount. And this relationship did not reduce the distance between them, inwardly it remained, and the consequence was, as the myths show, not a true marriage producing many good fruits of the spirit for the human partner; not man was raised but the divine was debased. Marriage with divinity produced in fact the prostitution ceremonies and the orgies of the fertility rites. There was no question of true love here.

That is the reason why paganism never broached the ideal of chastity. If in the service of certain divinities it insisted on the physical purity of the priest, and especially of the priestess, the reason was a sex taboo. Even Judaism never grasped the notion of chastity, though in a line with its exalted conception of a God high above all human concerns; but it only developed a sketchy form of sex taboo because in a world created by the one God, spiritual and good, there could be no naturally evil elements.

Christianity on the contrary was from the very beginning a religion of chastity, and it is precisely as such, though the fact is too often forgotten, that it endowed marriage with a new dignity and infused married intercourse with an intimacy and tenderness it had never known before. With Christian chastity something quite new appeared in the world, something which appears incomprehensible to a non-Christian. Christ himself drew attention to this: 'That conclusion, he said, cannot be taken in by everybody, but only by those who have the gift' (Matt. 19. 11).

So the time has come to examine the connection between this new thing and the fundamental novelty of Christianity: the incarnation of God. For it is in this connection that Christian chastity has its *raison d'être* and its true meaning. Now at last man can understand God without doing as the heathen did, mistaking him for something all too human.[1]

Acknowledgement of the Man Christ, in whose genuinely human behaviour and feeling the perfection of divine love is revealed for all to see, can inflame human hearts to such love and devotion to the God Man. His sublime form can take such complete possession of a man's thoughts and feelings, that there is no room left in him for that intimate attachment to another person which constitutes marriage. Chastity is thus essentially a special vocation to this all-inclusive love for God incarnate. In this vocation it resembles the ideal form of marriage, where each of two people is strongly and utterly convinced that the other is the only right one and there can be no other, to whom one will and must belong for ever. It is just as comprehensive a love as married love, more so actually, as we shall see. But as love for the God Man it is pure, pure not only in the narrower sense which makes every thought of sexuality in this connection a blasphemy, but also as a stern challenge to cast away all egoism and refuse ever to twist love into a means of self-assertion. For reverence for Christ's divinity and human perfection warrants a declaration of total war on self-love.

---

[1] Cf. A. Brunner, *Glauben und Erkenntnis*, 1951, Chap. 7.

Christ's life and mission teach us that God is pure love and that man can only come into contact with him and be bound close to him if he makes efforts to enter upon this selfless state through union with Christ. Pure and intimate both at once, this chaste virginal love for Christ has from the beginning been called bridal love.

This love implies a great intimacy with Christ, a familiarity which could hardly arise if man knew God only as pure Spirit. It is Christ as Man whom we picture with our mind's eye, with increasing actuality and verisimilitude. Through daily intercourse with him in prayer, Christ's ideas will gradually replace our own, tainted with sin. As a bride dwells in thought with her beloved, and lays all her plans in regard to him alone, and he becomes the climate in which she lives, so shall Christ be the whole room 'in all its breadth and length and height and depth' (Eph. 3. 18) in which the loving soul is increasingly at home. To please him: that is the only reward the loving soul requires, to share his joys, his sufferings. Chastity is intimate communion with Christ in selfless love. In this love the feelings are not deadened but clarified from within. Bridal love is love with all the strength of spirit and heart. It is a heartfelt love that grows ever more intimate, stronger, clearer.

CONCERN FOR WHAT IS THE LORD'S

Just as a bride's love extends to include all that is dear to her promised spouse—his family, previously unknown to her but through the power of love to become her own: so will chaste love for Christ extend to all that he loves (1 Cor. 7. 32 ff.). Therefore all are brothers and sisters in Christ and are to be loved unselfishly for his sake. Thus the extended egoism of family or group is overcome. And of all people, it is the poor and little ones who are Christ's favourites. So it is no accident that the works of Christian charity and the education of children were from the very beginning the special charge of those committed to chastity, and the Christian priesthood is closely linked to it. What cannot be done for Christ in his mortal life is done for his Body living on in the world, in the certainty that what is done to one of the least of the brethren is done for him (Matt. 25. 40). In addressing itself to the appointed works of spiritual and bodily assistance, the chaste soul finds its own place in the system of set forms that life cannot do without, but avoids losing itself in imaginations and self-delusions.

Chastity brings with it a great obligation to love other people. It promotes the serious effort to love people unselfishly, with no concern for any possible pleasure or advantage to be gained from their society, and no attention paid to any purely instinctive attraction or repulsion that may be felt, nor any care for whether this affection will contribute to the fulfilment of one's own emotional life. All the opportunities for egoism that always lurk in human relations, poisoning even family life from without and within, should be countered with increasing firmness, by keeping one's gaze constantly fastened on Christ.

What has to happen is practically a miracle—it is beyond unredeemed human powers: to be unselfish without being cold in feeling, to love dearly and yet not seek oneself and one's own pleasure in this love. Love for the high stature of Christ, who stands before the human soul as Man and God, makes such love possible by mightily raising a man above himself. He whose heart is brimming with such love can venture to approach others with warm love without running the risk of entanglement. Chaste love achieves on this plane what married love should bring about in relations with other people: that sexual desires and temptations be permanently banished from them. It is not the warmth of personal attraction that should disappear or give way; on the contrary—but it must burn with a clear flame.

The chaste soul is not without a family: in the members of Christ's family it has people to care for, just as man and wife do for their own offspring. But it does so for Christ's sake. Blood relationships are replaced by the spiritual bonds of self-denying love. These new bonds are not weaker but stronger and unite people over and beyond all natural differences into a new family, the family of Christ (Matt. 12. 46–50), and constitute a new people whose posterity is not by natural descent but by the spiritual regeneration of baptism (Rom. 9).

All those differences due to birth, status, education and whatever else there may be that determines whether a man makes a good impression or not among his fellows, must pale before the dignity of being a brother or sister of Christ's, which is everyone's portion (Matt. 25. 31–46). Our neighbour is not necessarily our near relation or our personal friend: these are natural distinctions that no longer hold. Rather it is helping, healing love that turns anyone into our neighbour by sustaining him in his need (Luke 10. 30 ff.). Envy and jealousy, which so often poison life in common, must be silenced through devotion to Christ; he who truly loves Christ can only rejoice when fortune smiles on the activities of the brothers and sisters and their endeavours are so much ready witness for Christ.

In the light of faith every human form should be transparent and

Christ's countenance show radiant in every human face, however dis-
figured it may otherwise be. When this happens, then the world of
men, so addicted to the temptation to love falsely and hate mortally,
will once more become the intermediary of the loving presence of
God in Christ. The spirit of poverty revives that awareness of the
creative love of God in things, and in chastity the redeeming love of
God which appeared in human form in Christ is again apparent, shining out to us from every human face. Thus the most important and
foremost field of all is reconquered for God's kingdom: that of our
fellow men.

Now, is it a fact that in Christian love, when a man is loved not for
his own sake but for Christ's, he is only serving as an occasion for love,
or is possibly only the object of our charity on the lookout for merits?
If it were so, man were merely a disguised form of tool once more,
though for the sake of Christ and Christians. Any man with a sense
of human dignity could but decline such love as this. It is an objection
that has often been raised. Were it correct, then Christian love were no
longer the highest of all values and might well be rejected as injurious
to human dignity.

Actually the objection does not touch true Christian love, but only
certain forms of behaviour which resemble it in outward appearance
but lack its spirit. We must be clear in our minds about this: spiritual
things are not self-contained and mutually exclusive like material things.
Love is the capacity to place oneself in the position of another, as one's
fellow, without displacing his own unique self by our intrusion:
rather, through love the other will receive confirmation of his individuality, and receive it in a manner appropriate to himself. But when
someone is loved merely because of some excellence he has which is
truly *his* but is no longer *him*, then high love lowers itself and the slip
is the greater, the more external and accidental the quality in question
is. This person can only be reached through love for a moment at a
time. And in sensual love this risk of slipping is always imminent.

But if it is true that human personality issues from God's creative
love, and only exists because God constantly maintains it in existence,
then a glance and an attitude that size up a man and endorse him in his
deepest depths cannot fail to come upon those deep springs of his being.
And the place where they issue is still essentially personal. Love of a
man will therefore involve the same love of those depths that the man
himself should have for them; love of the creative love at work there.
And this holds even when—specially when—the man does not love

them himself, knowing nothing about issuing from God. Yet to love the place to which he owes the mainspring of his being would be to his own utmost advantage, freely and of a purpose establishing him at last in those depths of self where he belongs. Now the process of endorsing the total potentialities of a man requires the kind of love we were speaking of, loving him in God and as issuing from God.

This love is not offered him in order to seize a desired opportunity for doing good or as a sure means for bringing him to love God— that is, as a means that can be put to use now and dropped later on. It is far nearer the truth to say that a man can only be wholly loved, as his being deserves, when he is loved and affirmed from his depth of origin upwards, from the very sources of his selfhood. And this love enters into the creative love of God, and what it affirms is the creature of its creation. In a sense, love has a share in the creation of the beloved, and by the affirmation of his existence it has a share in restoring to him his own base. When love does not press onward to these depths, then it is not offered to the whole man and is not yet the greatest love possible.

This eternal base of individual being has only been perceptible to man in Christ. The heathen did not believe their gods to be the creators of the world and the sources of individual existence. Only through revelation do we know of creation, that creation done out of nothing by the love of God. And what such creation means can only be understood to the full in selfless love. Yet to attain to this man had first to be redeemed by Christ. Thus it is only through union with Christ that redeemed man can bend down into the depths of another man, just as it is only in Christ himself that he reaches God in the authenticity of his personal Being. Only in Christ can he understand those depths humanly, that is to say, being love, understand them lovingly. Love for the Man Christ attains by mysterious means to the personal Being of God because the Man Christ is the same as the Word, the divine Person. In Christ it does really come to the beloved's base of being, and in him alone. Therefore ultimate, perfect, pure love to a human being is only possible as love in Christ.

Besides, through its inclusion in the Godhead Christ's humanity is in a special relationship to each man, that is, to his deepest depths. Without any merging into an impersonal union, Christ is deeply and lovingly attached to each and at one with each. He knows each one perfectly, as the Father knows him and he the Father (John 10. 14–15). No one is a stranger to him. His voice is familiar to all and is audible in places where no human voice penetrates (John 10. 1–10). Thus he could say: 'Believe me, when you did it to one of the least of my brethren here, you did it to me' (Matt. 25. 40). Selfless love for a man, when it drives on down to these depths, meets Christ himself there, Christ who in his redeeming love accepts to be on the same footing as his creature. Thus every true love for a man is love of him in Christ, even when he is ignorant of this mystery. In this love he is loved as created and redeemed through the love of God, and thus his whole being receives affirmation. That is why it is the highest love possible. It loves a man not less but more. He is not just a means to an end, a method of access, but the object of a love that drives on down to where no other love can reach. A world-bound and hence a lesser love, which yet intends to love as powerfully and completely as can possibly be done, may deem that love in Christ strikes through a man and beyond him into the distance: it cannot know that what it takes for distance is really the authentic depth of the man himself. And such a striking through and beyond a man is not a possibility; for to drive on as far as can be done is to reach God as a man's Creator and Redeemer, and there can be no more question of distance. The final dividing walls between man and man disappear here at last when they discover their common source of origin. Till that point is reached, their two beings remain, as from the beginning, independent of one another and alien to one another, and love it is that runs up against this persistent alienation and suffers from it. That is where the miracle takes place, for their two personalities do not merge pantheistically, as the heathen believed, and disappear; and yet, through the fulfilment of their selfhood in the love of God in Christ, this alienation too is done away with, together with the last traces of loneliness.

If chastity is thus lived, then it must produce a splendid enrichment of the soul. It deepens the soul's capacity for love to an inconceivable degree. For loving Christ alone, it experiences none of the disappointment that accompanies all earthly love even in its fulfilment. No earthly love can quench the longing of the human heart. The more intense it is, the more imperiously does it point beyond itself. Not in the sense of being otherwise left behind, but because it has a vocation to direct the heart towards eternal love, where alone all love between people finds its ultimate fulfilment. Chaste love goes straight on to this eternal love, by-passing the usual human intermediaries.

But it does go through a man, though it is the Man in whom eternal love became flesh. Love for this Man has no limits for it leads directly into the boundless depths of God. It is no accident that it is in Christianity that man's whole capacity for love first flowered. And this revelation was brought about by chastity. To it marriage owes the fact that it has become something deeper and more intimate than it was among the heathen; that it did not remain merely a matter of sexual intercourse and a bond for economic and social reasons, but also, and increasingly, became a spiritual relationship between two people with equal rights. Chastity set marriage free to become something more dignified and human, and it has to go on striving for this end through the example of pure love for Christ. The freedom thus gained has been particularly favourable to women. The Christian virgins were the first to break down the state of bondage that social custom laid upon women. A girl was married in accordance with family interests. There was no escaping from this compulsion. The virgins who paid for their Christian vocation with the sacrifice of their lives opened up the way of freedom for their sisters. And today the greater respect and veneration paid to women as the weaker sex come from the same attitude. Where Christianity with its high estimation of chastity loses ground, respect for the dignity of woman disappears too.

The chaste life places before the married a goal that it is just as important for them to reach as those committed to chastity. Spirit and body have to be set free from entanglement in sex, which reduces the spirit to the status of a tool and would drag it down to its own selfish ends. Man must be released from its inexorable grasp if he is, in all peace and devoid of egoistical desires, to meet someone of the opposite sex not as a specimen of that sex but as a human being.

When people come together, the dominating element should not be something that is *not* man's distinguishing or individual feature. It is not a question of getting free from the body but of freeing the body by increasing the power of the spirit that gives soul to the body. The body should rise to the level of the spirit and yet remain body—instead of the spirit being dragged down into the depths of sexuality with its demon of seduction. By a new way, by way of the redemption, the state of man in paradise is to be sought for afresh. In this sense Christian marriage too should produce chastity of soul. At the final goal the two ways meet—it could not be otherwise.

TRUE LOVE

Here, too, the spiritual and human enrichment appears first in the guise of impoverishment, and the extended scope of love as an imposition of loneliness. For in the foreground of consciousness there linger those selfish feelings which are so narrowly connected with sexuality; for most people, after all, love means the comfortable sense of being loved, rather than true love. And in love based on chastity these feelings remain without nourishment and die a slow and painful death of starvation. But meanwhile, weak in comparison and hard to identify, in the inmost depths, in the very core of being, the new, selfless love is growing all the while, but among the noisy chatter of those other foreground feelings its low voice is almost inaudible. True life will be felt as a bitter death-blow to what is most human in us. And the danger is great that the heart will not be able to bear its solitude. To rid itself of pain it is tempted to grow hard, to deaden feeling, or simply to give up trying to make the effort to love. But a hardening of the heart must never be allowed except as an unavoidable temporary measure or a defence in time of danger. A display of stoical apathy towards human sensibility is no Christian solution. It ignores the characteristic feature of chastity. And on its account a man would never be the richer but only the poorer. So that is no proper means to perfection; it misses out love, which is that in which perfection consists.

Celibacy as such does not constitute chastity. There are a number of reasons for choosing a non-married life. Anyone who keeps clear of marriage in order to lead a comfortable existence unburdened by family cares, with the ego firmly planted in the centre of the picture, is not expanding his humanity to embrace new opportunities. Christian chastity is essentially service done to the Body of Christ, whether through prayer and penance in the name of all our fellow men and women, or through the works of charity. Only thus does it perform its duty towards society, as a reminder to married people of where the point of gravity in marriage should lie: in union over high human and personal matters, in the union of selfless being-for-one-another.

Thus a man will discover that he cannot use another person as his exclusive property, as a thing belonging to him and existing only for him. That is the nature-bound attitude of bodily life, for which spiritual life is of no account. What is called love is often no more than an intemperate desire for total possession of the other person, not even consenting to let this other person keep the incontrovertible freedom which is everyone's portion. But whatever is physical is suppressive and exclusive; to be body or to be essentially bound to a body is to be subject to this law, and indeed rightly so within its own range. Whereas nothing spiritual is reduced in quantity by being shared among many, and to endow one spiritually is not to deprive the rest, as where body and matter are concerned. The desire to possess exclusively, rooted in bodily life, tends however in mankind to spread to the spiritual life. In every human being there lurks the urge to make a slave of the other person, who is taken possession of, like a thing—and man dares to call that act of piracy love!

Thus it is 'natural' for people to be on the defensive with one another. They live in perpetual fear of being exploited and taken advantage of. And this fear is not without valid grounds. It is the natural attitude of unredeemed man who takes it for granted that he is the centre-point of the world. Like the beasts, each on meeting his fellow sums him up, estimating his strength, reckoning on his weaknesses, so as to make good use of both for his own advancement. This is an attitude worthy of beasts of prey and introduces into human relations a very disquieting element and a tendency to adopt rigidly defensive positions. But above all it drives the most individual and deepest part of man into hopeless isolation, eliminating all possibility of genuine love. The very fact of being attached to a body limits the possibilities of complete openness and transparency towards one another. But the way to one another is made much harder through the natural mistrust of one egoism over against another.

Moreover this jealous desire to possess exclusively is foredoomed to failure.[1] For it is contradictory to want to bind someone else's freedom to oneself without suppressing it. The beloved one is supposed to succumb to a sort of spell and submit in every respect. But that is the end of being human, i.e. of being in a position to live of free accord with and for others in love. It is reducing a person to a mere thing to be pushed around at will. Any notion of the fulfilment and joy which other-ness guarantees, and alone guarantees, collapses entirely. The beloved one is indifferent. Thus it is fulfilment itself that eludes those who seek it acquisitively, and possessive desire is *ipso facto* self-destructive. This explains how it is that mere sensual love, which always contains an element of possessiveness, so easily turns into hatred and to the will to destroy the deceptive object of its love, as a sort of proof of frustrated ownership, even though the way to positive ownership has been missed. But any sensitive nature is bound to feel wounded and degraded on being required to yield utterly and surrender selfhood itself. Such an one will close and refuse and put up defences in horror

[1] Cf. J.-P. Sartre, *L'être et le néant.*

and hatred. Sensual and spiritual love in man go opposite ways and tear him apart so long as sensual love is not caught into human wholeness by a strong spiritual love; then, shedding its dictatorial claims, it becomes amenable to serve a true being-for-one-another.

Man can only really bind himself to selfless love. For this alone respects his selfhood and does not attempt to turn him into a tool of the other person's self-assertiveness. Only love is not concerned with dominating and exploiting; only love is not out for itself. Therefore where love is man feels secure and his defensive attitude relaxes. Thus love melts down that stiffening of envy and mistrust and life ceases to be one ruthless struggle for existence. Love alone holds the key to the inmost stronghold of the souls of others. Its effect goes straight to the bottom, to those depths whence men's motives and actions spring. And the remarkable thing is that love, asking for nothing, not rating itself in terms of assets for the ego, not on the look-out for itself—love it is that is most potent in transforming people. For it has access to what is otherwise closed to all else.

But it achieves this mighty transformation in apparent impotence. Or rather in very real impotence wherever ambition and push are paramount, that is to say, in the only spheres that count where the current conception of reality has no relation to redemption. Faced with this impotence of love, the self-seeking ego crumbles away. Thus true love appears as a rejection of self and loss of self, as spiritual death. It is not for nothing that the uttermost and deepest extreme of self-being is called selflessness; for what a man usually considers to be himself is the obtrusive noisy self of egoism, and this must give way if love is to have room. Only God loves with pure selflessness, as is his nature; for only God needs nothing and therefore seeks nothing outside himself. But from this very fact it is clear that the impotence of selflessness must rest on the spiritual and personal power of selfhood. God's love credits all things with the right to be and does not find any of them in the way. Thus all are open to him. And no one accords more respect to man's selfhood than God does. He does not use it like a thing. He lets man enjoy the freedom that belongs to his being and the self-determination proper to him. He uses no compulsion, not even when man's own happiness is at stake—knowing that happiness is inseparably linked to freedom of selfhood and that it is a senseless undertaking to try to make someone happy against his will. So God leaves a man his will, even to do evil; not out of indifference, but in order that he may freely win through to himself. His grace is at hand at every moment, to help him to make good use of his freedom to promote his happiness.

The regard with which God treats man is such that in the world's eyes his power appears as impotence, and things pursue their course as though there were no God. Evil asserts itself as the real power in this world, as its prince (John 12. 31), and all the amenities of civilization and culture are at its disposal. It makes such strides and takes such full command of the immediate scene that man begins to doubt God's existence and to despair of the power of good. Exploitation, the ruthless struggle for existence and the possession of worldly goods, appear to be the sole powers of human history, and in this struggle it is not as a rule the higher cause that wins, but sheer physical and economic force. And God remains silent. As a description of the foreground of history, marxist materialism is largely correct and many instances can be cited to corroborate it. The life-theories see force and resistance as the only props of reality: to show no capacity or desire to use force is to be non-existent.

But this is only a superficial view. Were these forces the sole lords of history, man would have been engulfed long ago. But other powers are at work, in all quietness, countering the powers of destruction. Quietly and in silence God is at work out of the depths of being. And nothing can escape his power. Evil has to set up an immense display of force and bombast and to indulge in relentless expenditure of energies, suspecting all the while how powerless it really is and how, despite all the fury of the attack, the decisive depths are safe from its encroachments. The more openly force rules relations between people, the more intractably those spheres remain closed to it, the ones that ultimately matter. God's silence is only the reverse side of a power sure of itself, never too late in action, never to be outplayed, for it is present the whole time. But it is present in the form of creative love.

As the revelation of this pure personal power, Christ appeared in earthly weakness and impotence. Not by means of force, not by enticement or deception, not through the influence of his family nor by political measures did he call to souls, but through the selflessness that radiates in all his deeds and words. But this selflessness met with blank incomprehending rejection and hatred. The fact that it did not turn into bitterness and disparagement is a revelation of the ineffable power of divine love, which loves without asking for return. Thus the love of Christ showed itself to be the strongest force in history, but always as a power veiled in outward impotence. Man has again and again to be pulled back from the desire to obtain domination over others, even when the intention is to make those others happy. It cannot be too often repeated: only he can influence other men's hearts who is not seeking to do so, working on other men for their good is God's preserve. For He alone has free access to a man's innermost soul. Men have intimate influence on one another only to the degree that they are selflessly open to God's action through them. In marriage, too, the couple only really possess one another when they let go of their egoistical desire to own and rule in order to live with one another and for one another. Only when love is such that the other person is free to be himself do the ultimate depths become tractable. Selfless love is also the key to true education and upbringing and to all work for the cure of souls.

But fallen man being what he is, he only attains to this selfless attitude towards another through apparent failure. For only in failure is it clearly seen whether what he is asking for is his own success, grooming his skill to prove his ability, or solely the good of his fellows. Failure calls for a painful process of readjustment and turns the mind to focus on the true end of all work, releasing it from the entanglements of a submerged power complex. In a world of egoism selfless love can expect nothing but injustice and exploitation. Christ himself could not evade them, not in spite of, but because of being selfless love in person. Indeed to an egoistical humanity such selflessness can only be understood as provocative mystification and deadly danger. But the Christian is not to be embittered or discouraged by all this. In the heavy hours of temptation he finds consolation in the Lord whose earthly life also apparently ended in the total failure of his whole work, not only among the masses but among the apostles too. Beneath the cross there stood only one young man and a few women. One of his own had betrayed him. Peter, his future deputy, had been ashamed and afraid and had denied him. The ruin of his life's work seemed to be total. But out of it all there arose that great thing which shall never die, and which has brought strength and consolation to millions in the darkest hours of their lives.

Of course human society cannot suddenly discard the use of force. Man is no pure spirit and outward material things make such pressing claims that it is impossible to rely on the good will of everyone all the time. Any menace to life and freedom arising through unjust use of force must be countered with force, unless preventive measures can be set on foot; otherwise our common ordered life and the growth of civilizations would be out of the question.

But it would be shocking to try to found all human relations on force. Even in external matters where force is in place, loyalty and faith, goodness and kindness must provide the real basis of human relations and exert growing influence for peace and reconciliation, if life is to be at all bearable. In the animal, force is strictly governed by instinct. In man it swells to ghastly proportions the moment it is given a little rope, and assumes the right to satisfy all the demands of man's being. Only an even stronger counter power can leash it up again and keep it within proper bounds; and this power is benevolent goodness. Every good man or woman is a prop for human society even without knowing it.

Abundant and manifold as they are, human qualities too stand wide open to the selfless approach. Egoism only gives other people a chance when it is to its own advantage, or at least no obstacle to it. On meeting anyone, the first question is: will he add to my prestige or prejudice my case? There is no question of letting him go his own way with detachment, though this is the only condition for seeing him as man in his own right and unique. So it never dawns on the egoistical mind how wonderfully variegated the human make-up is. It fails to remark how man can be man without having to conform to the pattern it imposes. Only by leaving man free to be himself in what is unique and special about him, is any vision possible of how rich the opportunities are. But this attitude must not be mistaken for indifference, which is only another form of egoism. It is rather an explicit recognition of the rights of the other man to be himself, to be what he is and realize his potentialities without having to wait for our approval. Physical life is narrowly concentrated on its own advantage and that of the species and indeed needs to be so because of its vulnerability and fragility. But spirit does not require to hedge itself in so narrowly and prudently. And above all not the man rooted in love, who knows that he is forever secure in love. If poverty sharpens the eye to take in the beauty and splendour of things, chastity does the same for the world of men. Where the prejudiced view sees only matter for dislike, disparagement and hatred, Christian love will look below the surface and find even here, buried away in the filth and rubbish, the eternal worth and incontrovertible dignity of God's creature, of Christ's redeemed. And if someone is young enough in spirit to remain capable of spotting and recognizing new values, then selfless love is the means by which man is exempt from the inexorable law of growing old—not in body but in spiritual life.

ANTICIPATING TRANSFIGURATION

But in its deepest sense Christian chastity can be termed an anticipation of transfiguration. This proves anew how little antagonism to the body is intrinsic to it. Since the appearance of original sin, the body is the obstacle to perfect presence and pure love. This is not only due to the egoism of sexuality but, as we saw, to its very nature, for its existence is conditioned by matter and is matter-bound. Now matter is dense, non-transparent and self-contained. It knows nothing outside itself; whatever happens to it happens regardless of consequences. It behaves as the total situation determines at any given moment. This incommunicability and impenetrability of matter is somewhat relaxed when life is present. And the link with the spirit brings light and freedom into the body itself. But nowadays it is beyond the power of spirit entirely to dispel the darkness and reduce the stiffness. On this account, in all human relations there remains not merely the fact of being different, which is in order, but a foreignness and impenetrability that block the way to perfect love. That is why total presence on another person's behalf is so rare and always so short-lived.[1] We are half absent, and often more than half, caught aside by pangs of greed or fear. We listen with half an ear if there is nothing afoot to benefit ourselves. The body is both the necessary medium of any human presence and contrives to impede and hamper this presence. Thus, even through love, two people can never totally enter one another's inmost being to find one another in the deepest depth of spirit.

Man has always been conscious of this deficiency in all human love. But finding himself powerless to remove the disparity through more intensive spiritualization of the body, he adopted the opposite method of shedding it from his consciousness (at least), treating the spirit as corporeal: he sought forgetfulness in states of intoxication and in the arid wastes of sheer sexuality. Moreover, as regards that ultimate union which man does in fact yearn for, a number of philosophical systems have found no better way of defining it than as the disappearance of individuality and the submergence of personality in an impersonal pantheistic universality. Indeed, in terms of matter, shedding individual being would be the only means of getting rid of separateness and dif-

[1] Cf. A. Brunner, *Der Stufenbau der Welt*, Chap. 4.

ferentness. But in the spiritual sphere that is not the way to attain to union. For the disappearance of personal being would involve the irretrievable ruin of that happiness which such union was expected to bring about, at the very moment of its incipience: there is no longer a person present to be able to be happy. Happy union rests in mutually promoted love rising from the very springs of their being when two people love one another. Not that they cease to be two, but unlike two mutually exclusive objects wholly alien in nature, they are two with a common well-spring for all they do and stand for. But this transference into the heart of another being is only perfect when utterly transparent. Transparent and self-transferable is the spirit alone. Therefore shedding the alienating elements for the sake of pure and perfect love would involve the total spiritualization of the body, quickening its transfiguration and hastening its adoption into the spiritual world.

It is of course impossible for man as he now is to undergo any such soul-infusion of the body. And that is why perfect love is denied him. There is only one real exception: it is the Man Christ. His human spirituality has its centre not in himself but in God; not bound to God as a human person, but directly in its being, as itself, belonging to a divine person. This spirituality is intrinsically connected with perfect possession of the body. As a consequence transfiguration is a state natural to the body. And only out of love for man and for the purpose of his redemption did Christ refrain from letting his divinity be evident in his body as long as he was here on earth (Phil. 2. 5 ff.). Nonetheless he had a power of presence unequalled by any other man. He was totally present to whomsoever approached him. And thus in every man he immediately touched the spot that hurt and healed it. But since the resurrection he lives as the transfigured Christ who has planted in his body the characteristic features of the spirit: 'The spirit we have been speaking of is the Lord' (2 Cor. 3. 17). Now, pure transparency and union to the deepest depths of personality meet with no more obstacles at all, and Christ can love everyone and no one can love like him. For him and him alone, there is no sense of estrangement, no dividing wall; he knows his own with that same perfect knowledge by which Father and Son are known to one another; and mankind knows him in so far as it is his and loves him (John 10. 7-15).[1]

Love for Christ in chastity anticipates the possibility of loving someone wholly and fully, and already here below man can seek to

[1] Cf. R. Guardini, Der Herr, 1937, pp. 208 ff.

base his life on this total relationship. If only to be done in faith and hope it is not on that account illusory, but is genuinely and deeply real, if but faintly apprehended through the heavy curtain of a man's still non-transfigured body. Spiritual intercourse with Christ leads naturally to that clarity and limpidity of soul that has less and less to conceal from the eyes of other people. Such a man meets his fellow men with increasing sincerity and candour, and through the power of Christ's spirit living in him, is able to plunge deeply into the hidden places of another's soul without any trace of violence done or any fear that to be subject to such insight is in any way degrading or shameful. In the lives of the saints a wonderful knowledge of what lies hidden in human hearts is no rare attribute. We need only think of the Curé d'Ars, so near to our own times—St. Jean Vianney.

Moreover transfiguration is anticipated in the increasing appease-ment of natural human instincts through the working of the spirit. 'The man who unites himself to the Lord becomes one spirit with him' (1 Cor. 6. 17). He lives out of depths where he is in contact with Christ and this brings order into all his personal motives, powerfully though without compulsion and without effort.

The average man finds his centre of gravity in the superficial levels of his being. That is why he does not succeed in harmonizing the manifold aspirations which arise from the various levels of his being, nor in heading them naturally towards that ultimate union. Indeed he himself is nowhere near it. He is torn in all directions by his various appetites and all too easily loses control. He is more or less a stranger to himself, determined by things that are not himself, and he is there-fore a stranger to his fellow men too. As spiritual power increases, whether through true married love or through love for Christ in chastity, it becomes gradually easier and less strenuous to achieve that unity which is an essential feature of personality; in spite of the Fall, man has a vocation to this unity, even though he can no longer attain to it by his own unaided powers. The body becomes more and more individual to its owner; that part-estrangement of the body from the personality, which is the foremost hallmark of the body, is transformed into an increasing intimacy of correspondence with the person; the penetration of the body by the soul will not be complete till transfigur-ation has occurred, when the body will be pliable to every wish and signal of the spirit, with no resistance and no cross-purposes. The final aim is not release from the body and matter, but release of the body through release of the spirit. Not till it is transfigured is body wholly body, for then at last it belongs to a man wholly, without resistance or estrangement. Then the whole man, body and soul, is radiant with transparency and glows with the power to love perfectly, as described in the 21st chapter of the Apocalypse in a variety of scenes which, for all their rapture, still remain far short of what redeemed and transfigured man will really be like.

According to all this, the secret of chastity, its nature and significance lie in its special relation to the incarnation. It is enrolment in the response of the Man Christ to adoption by God. To express it in inadequate human terms, it is as though the human nature of Christ was swept up into the Godhead in such a mighty surge of love that it resolved not to be a separate individual person, so as to achieve the adoption of the creature by God in the most perfect way possible: something far beyond all human capacity. In reality union of the human nature of Christ with the Person of the Word occurred before ever human will desired it, for the desire did not exist before and was created in the union. But this renunciation of separate individual personality received immediate acknowledgement and acceptance. 'As Christ comes into the world, he says, No sacrifice, no offering was thy demand: thou hast endowed me with a body. Thou hast not found any pleasure in burnt sacrifices, in sacrifices for sin. See then, I said, I am coming to fulfil what is written of me, where the book lies unrolled; to do thy will, O my God' (Heb. 10. 5 ff.). Through love for Christ the chaste soul is swept up into this mighty current of self-surrender: for it too no longer wants to live of itself and for itself but only for God in Christ. Christ will be the divinely human centre of its life, a hearth from which it turns towards whatever life may bring and goes out to meet it.

When a man so closely approximates to this centre, the heart of Jesus, that he is actually living from a centre of his own which is not his own, he is fulfilling the words of the Apostle Paul: 'I am alive, or rather, not I, it is Christ that lives in me' (Gal. 2. 20); this is the purpose of every Christian life, and particularly of life in chastity.

Indeed, for humanity to be taken up into God through Christ is the final goal of all life and its deepest meaning; here is no pantheistic submergence and elimination but personal self-surrender out of love for him. In chastity it is the explicit target, through the bond with the Man Christ in pure and holy love. And as our Lord was not less man than other men, but rather, more; and as he was wholly and yet simply and plainly man, self-surrender through love will not do away with personality but lead it towards its final perfection. Indeed the saints, and among them again most visibly the splendid women of Church history, testify to the truth of this: in a unique combination of tenderness and strength, feminine reticence and manly audacity in the most breath-taking schemes, they display strength without harshness and tenderness without weakness. From all sorts of new angles they reflect him whom they loved and to whom all was brought in sacrifice: their Lord Jesus Christ, our own Lord.

CHAPTER FOUR

Freedom and Obedience

SELF-WILL AND GOD'S WILL

THROUGH poverty man is relieved of excessive care for outward things and of the ensuing craving for more and more possessions: things are restored to their rightful place and God is found in them. Chastity cleanses human relations of the sexual strains that tend to poison them and quenches the lust for pleasure or power, enabling people to be really present to one another in love and through and beyond this to live in God's presence.

But it can easily happen that in spite of all a man still remains isolated, finding merely new and stronger self-endorsement and enhanced pleasure in his own powers. Through abnegation a man increases the scope of his freedom, that is, of his real individual self: he rises above the human average. Deliberately acquired independence of things that make slaves of other men, and an ill-defined awareness of mental powers hardly understood in ordinary life, constitute one of the most dangerous temptations of all: a new form of self-seeking, not the less perverted for being on the spiritual plane: the danger of pride and self-adulation. This man needs gods no more, for he is his own god, not in his transient bodily form but in his sense of being inwardly free and independent of the outside world—in his perception of his own superiority. This is the state for which the yogi strives, by means of asceticism raising himself above the gods to the intimate conviction that the whole world rests in his power. Not crude unspiritual physical power, but the farthest and highest reaches of the human mind. That is what is worshipped: the individuality of man.

It is immediately evident that this sort of pride is at the farthest point possible from Christian perfection. For it is a state of mind in which man is least inclined and least able to bow down before God and in love deliver over to him his own will, his own most intimate self. It is the pride that is the devil's own sin, the insurrection of the creature against its Creator, an ultimate and profound refusal to serve him. It is far worse than any form of acquisitiveness or pleasure-seeking, where at bottom people are always more or less conscious of their wretchedness and can still find their way back from that point. Publicans and prostitutes are nearer to the kingdom of heaven than the self-righteous pharisee (Matt. 21. 31 ff.; Luke 18. 9 ff.).

This pride is not found in its crasser form in a man endeavouring to lead a Christian life. But it is all the more prevalent in its more secretive and refined forms. Every man is proud of what he can do. His achievements are means of self-expression. His mind, his will-power and above all his capacity to put new things into the world as free products of his native wit, changing the world's course—are all in evidence in his successful ventures. And the more unique the stroke of genius, the more independent of all previous products, the more thorough the changes wrought—the greater is the human mind behind it all. The more confidently man asserts himself among the things of this world, the less he owes to his environment. And the more he is what he is: someone whose achievements place him in the public eye—the more powerful is his personality.

It is quite evident that awareness of being at the top of one's powers is one of the most exhilarating and stimulating states that man can attain to. It endorses his existence most forcefully, lifting him completely clear of that sense of insufficiency and frailty which is otherwise the normal undercurrent of human life, and planting him on his own ground. Never is man more conscious of his independence and superiority than in the hour of great achievement. And at the back of his strenuous activity, a craving for self-endorsement is the ulterior spring of action, all the more urgent and ardent the more a man detaches himself from the common motives of property and pleasure. A secret urge to find his life a firm reliable ground within himself drives him on relentlessly and has done so ever since through original sin he suffered the loss of conscious anchorage in the love of God. Since then, he knows his true origin only through faith, without being able to grasp it. So he turns the more readily to his own freedom, his own selfhood and his own mental powers for a solution. Each successive achievement is an endorsement of the fact that man with his sense of personal power is sufficient unto himself. 'Nothing succeeds like success'—hence that curious clear-headed state of intoxication with its accompanying enhanced consciousness where delusion can all the more easily slip in unobserved. With these subtle unadmitted strains of self-adulation all human attainment is tainted. It is that 'pride of life' (cf. 1 John 2. 16;

James 4. 16) that threatens man in the deepest depth of his being.[1] And it is precisely the great and magnanimous soul that is most precariously exposed to this temptation.

If man is the creature called into being out of nothingness by the creative word of God, then this attitude is exactly contrary to his nature and is therefore an error. Towards the heathen deities, who never claimed to have brought the world and man into existence out of nothing, but at the very most to have been the shapers of an already existing eternal reality, such an attitude of independence on the part of man was quite appropriate, for all the relative superiority of those divinities. But they could not, for instance, inspire any devotion in love, nor did their followers ascribe total world sovereignty to them. This sovereignty resided in the impersonal law of destiny which like the matter of the world was there from all times and was never created.

But as we know, man was made out of nothing; to God he owes his selfhood, the source of his whole capacity to produce anything new, as self-determining cause and origin. He is not planted upon himself, he is not the ultimate base of his own being. This base is moreover no more impersonal than he is. Were it impersonal, then there would be no question of obligations towards it, for it could not have created the world by a free act of will; issuing from such an impersonal base would be a purely natural and causal process with no call on man's gratitude or any other state of mind of his: no possibility of knowing it even. Were there really such a base to our being, the most dignified attitude for man to take up would be to accept what he could not alter, like the stoic who in proud indifference lets the inevitable break over him without uttering a word of complaint, thus affirming his superiority of spirit.

But the truth is otherwise. Human existence is the constantly given gift of a freely giving love, a personal love. With the consequence that created man, endowed with knowledge and freedom, is duty-bound freely to acknowledge this origin of his, and thus to establish contact with it, and this is done through worship and devoted love. When the creature enters lovingly into the will of the Creator and assents to it, he assents at the same time to his own existence and thus comes to terms with himself. When he gives back his own being unconditionally, from the very depths of himself gives it back to eternal love, then at last man attains to that deepest self of his and gains perfect control over himself. Thus in this worship of love he is wholly himself and wholly

[1] Pascal, *Pensées* (ed. Brunschvicg), 150, 153.

at one with his origin, as far as this is possible for a created being. And this coming to terms with one's own base of being, that is to say, with oneself, constitutes blessedness, it constitutes salvation. All attempts to reach perfection by other means are foredoomed to failure as running counter to reality. Rather all action should serve to promote total self-surrender. Freedom from all created things, because their ultimate fragility and impotence are admitted—yes; but in order to seek one's security under the wing of that absolute freedom from which one's own freedom continuously springs.

This ultimate surrender of self is natural to man as created and yet it is almost too difficult for man in original sin. For now he has no direct experience of that origin of his, since he turned away from it through sin, but he knows it only indirectly and darkly. Thus it seems to him he is stepping out into the void when he renounces himself to go home to God. What God requires of him seems to demand impossible sacrifices of him. Since the Fall, service to the true God has always appeared to man as something beneath his dignity; he has the impression he is simply throwing himself away, and playing fast and loose with what is most precious to him, never to be given away, or at most only to bestow on the beloved one, because contact here, in mutual giving, produces expansion of selfhood and not its loss. Service to the pagan gods was without this humiliating element; so is service to those substitute deities which in our modern western paganism supplant our true God. For here natural man, unredeemed, finds himself endorsed in what is most individual to him, in his supposed dignity and greatness. And indeed there is nothing here to challenge man's pride and make him refuse his services, for in this sort of worship he is more or less worshipping himself too, one way or another. He may be inferior to his gods, but he is part of the same cosmic set-up and has nothing particular to thank them for. And in the cult of country and nation, or science, or humanity, or civilization, man is doing honour to himself too. For at the source of all these there are forces that are directly related to him. To natural man it is quite in order to share in those cults and to bow to the superiority of such forces is highly admirable. It is not as though their greater powers put his lesser powers in question. However, that ultimate gift that our true God requires of us, and without which all the rest is worthless, is denied from this same standpoint as being too humiliating altogether. On that account it is impossible to approach Christianity in an attitude of tolerant indifference, like the other religions. It claims too much not to provoke the man who does not acknowledge it; for in spite of all he is fundamentally aware that it is right, and can see the radical difference between its claims and those of other religions. It is possible to see in them all, at various levels, in principle equally valid forms of religious views and claims, not mutually exclusive at all, where a man can choose whatever suits him best; all however leaving the innermost self untouched.

For all that, it is only total self-surrender to God that has the desired effect: God's will must be decisive in all things because man's own will receives from God all its power to will. The purpose of freedom can only be to acknowledge this fact and to bind oneself freely to the will of the Creator. As God alone is pure beginning and origin, and all man's capacity to be author and creator derives from him and displays the power of his freedom as a distant reflection, so is it the destiny of this finite origin to restore itself to the true ultimate origin and not to want to be anything but the instrument, alive and free, whereby God's love is given effect.

Pride, which is the natural reaction of a man to his own creative activities, must go deeper, must drive on down to the ultimate base and find there the pure causality of God. To himself as originator man should have nothing ascribed, neither by other people nor, least of all, by himself. But to God alone to whom indeed he owes his capacity to be an originator at all. He should not insist on himself, on his will, for without God he and his will would be nothing. Only in unconditional obedience to God's will, admitting in humility that he is only the penultimate, with God behind him as final ultimate, only thus is man free to be what he truly is: a creature of God's creation. Here at last he is alive to his deepest depths and is thus, against all appearances, more himself than when he depends on himself as an ultimate rooted in a sub-personal base. For where he deceives himself he is not the man he thought he was, that is, he is not wholly himself. Only in self-dedication to God does a man come to himself, and then at last what he takes himself to be corresponds to what he really is.

This is the meaning and purpose of existence, and to this every Christian life is committed. Whoever wants to be saved has to reach this state of obedience. And he will not be able to see God face to face so long as he is not prepared to recognize it. For to be face to face is a personal relationship and persons are only known when their selfhood is acknowledged. To be admitted to the blessed communion of God's absolute personal being postulates this unreserved and unconditional acknowledgement on the part of man, and Christianity demands it. In this ultimate ultimate there are no differences or degrees. Each man has to do the best he can according to his lights. So that differences occur only in the form of that act of utter dedication and surrender.

For a man who accepts the fact of creation out of nothing this requirement is not so hard to understand, however heavy-going the realization of it may be. In all situations man lives and acts as creature created by God. In all situations it is his duty to do what God requires of him here and now. The situation itself declares what God's will is. After all it did not come about against God's will or in spite of it. All that is can only really be through God's creative power. And in all that happens man should be aware of God as the causation, committing himself to it in loving trust, helping to give it effect in his own field. For man living in grace without original sin, this attitude would be taken for granted at every passing moment. Nor would he remain content with things as created causes; but secure in the love of good, he would be able to see all creatures, men and objects, as they really are and would accord them their due place; instead of merely considering them in relation to his own advantage, laying greedy hands upon them or fleeing from them in fear, as the case might be. He would clearly understand that in their causation God himself was at work and in their effect he would detect the voice of God telling him his will. In all occurrences, pleasant or unpleasant, God would be present to him and filled with loving trust he could give himself up to His will with neither fear nor reservation. Then he would not overlook created causes with their unique being; he would on the contrary give them a much more searching and comprehensive look: he would recognize them to be what they are, as continually receiving all being and all causation from their divine origin. A view of reality which is content with the finite causes of the world is in reality an incomplete view, an abstract one; and it becomes a lie when it claims to be an account of the whole of reality.

For the true view in the spirit of obedience, inner-worldly events no longer signify a distraction from God; rather they make him visible, as though through a veil. Considering how lightly veiled divine action in the world is, it ought not to be hard for man to understand his own activities as made possible by God; and hence to know that his own intentions can be no other than to accompany God's action totally and whole-heartedly in whichever direction it takes, and to assent to God's will without reserve in his own range of activities as made possible by God; and thus recognize him as First Cause from whom all causation issues.

But since through man's fault the living bond with his divine origin has been broken, the course of events no longer appears to man with such transparency. His view is blunter and looks no further than inside the world itself for causes. This is inevitable, seeing that he experiences his own selfhood as an absolute base; hence other inner-worldly causes, and above all other men, appear as existing in themselves. For they did not, he supposes, draw either their being or their function from one another, he did not get his from them nor they get theirs from him. The multiplicity of such final origins is illustrated by the multiple gods of paganism, but when philosophy advanced to the discovery of one single final cause, it still remained unreal and lifeless: more a mode of expression than an actual origin. Ordered all alike in being, these causes must mutually exclude and displace one another. Thus man's part is to see to himself, make his own way, keep his eyes open for the main chance, here, there and everywhere, and defend it against all comers. When his defence holds and his enterprises succeed, when his work is obviously superior and special, he feels confirmed in his being. And he needs to have this confirmation of himself constantly endorsed, for he is perpetually conscious of the insecurity of his being and keeps an eye on it all the time, however surreptitiously. Troubles may well make a man envious of his fellows and drive him into conflict with them, for he feels that he is being unfairly treated: they occupy space that is rightly his and cut him short of material goods. But the reason for it all is in great part anxiety for his own menaced existence, an anxiety that provokes him to push ahead at the cost of others, raise himself by reducing them, affirm his own strength by seeing to it that they are aware of their impotence. The passion for taking people down a peg has no other source but this, and the depth at which it is rooted makes it very difficult completely to eradicate it. It is not the quality of one's achievement that counts at this stage, but the superiority it bestows on one's person, bolstering up one's sense of security. But if another man's achievements are successful, for the same reason the fact will be seen as a menace and as detrimental to one's own powers. On that account the natural attitude of man to his fellow men is split, made up of hate-love. One needs people as rungs on the ladder of success and as a scale by which to measure one's own ability and skill. And then, in order to make them feel one's power, one degrades them and eliminates them. A poor sort of power, that can only work

destructively! It is hatred that makes conflicts between men so merci-
less, so infinitely gruesome, as they never are in the animal world where
rivalries arise merely over feeding and mating. The animal as such is
not cruel. It never hurts in order to hurt. In human conflicts over food,
pleasure or comfort something else creeps in, something diabolical,
which is the will to power, which seeks in the abasement and degradation and even elimination of fellow men a form of self-confirmation,
however transitory. Let there be no illusions, all humanism has this
vulnerable side to it. And the headlong lapses into utter barbarity that
our so progressive age has experienced are only surprising to those who
have a childishly unreal idea of the nature of man. Man strays all his
days over a hidden abyss where dread lurks, and this abyss is the void
of his own existence when he imagines he has to keep it going himself.

Here man is most truly and deeply lost. Here he can no longer find
his own way home; for self itself, the motivating self, is lost. Hence the
impossibility of saving himself. He has to be saved by someone who is
not always astray in pathless wastelands, someone whose living bond
with the source of things has never been broken. We know that the
God-Man Jesus Christ is the incarnate bond with God and that as Man
he drew his life from it. Only when man can enter into this bond anew
and be conscious of it can he extract himself—or rather be extracted—
from his entanglement in self-centred anxieties. Henceforth, reassured
as to his true origin, he will live to do God's will as manifest in Christ.

THE REVELATION OF THE WILL OF GOD

But here is the incomprehensible surprise for the world: this will
was not revealed, as heathendom and Judaism expected, in the form of
proud self-being and ruthless self-assertion: as a power striking its
opponents down, loudly triumphant over their downfall. No, but
'gentle and humble of heart' (Matt. 11. 29), selfless, self-denying even,
in the form of a man, a poor, powerless, humiliated man who fell an
easy prey to his enemies (Phil. 2. 6 ff.). He came to serve others, not to
have service done him (Matt. 20. 28; Mark 10. 45). That was the great
scandal; it was a smack in the face to all former conceptions of God as
irresistible power and avenging fire. A God who goes out to encounter
the foe with fire and lightning is easily understood in the light of
human greed. There is even a hope that his vindictiveness and self-
worship might be turned to good advantage by skilful flattery and
bribery, and the undoubted superiority in battle could be used to crush
and destroy a man's own private opponents. But egoism can make

nothing of a humble, weak, suffering God who ignominiously succumbs to his enemies. How was he to save others, when he could not
save himself (Matt. 27. 39 ff.; Mark 15. 29 ff.; Luke 23. 35)? How could
he possess power when he did not even use it to help himself? The Cross
of Christ was and is a folly and a scandal to the natural understanding
(1 Cor. 1. 23).

The will of God is thus something quite unlike what sinful man
supposes. And here arises another danger, an all too real danger as history shows. If each man is to give his own account of God's will in
given circumstances at any particular time, will he do it without error?
He has only got his egoistically tainted mind and will to do it with.
And egoism may well find a means of asserting its own will under
cover of the will of God. It is crafty enough to give a twist to objections, to simulate this or that genuine good as motive, and all the time
to be thinking only of itself. Hence ensues a positively monstrous
abuse. God's will and the will of man appear to coincide, as Christianity requires. But in actual fact the identification is reached by
measuring God's will to man's and debasing it into a tool of egoism.
Where this occurs, spiritual grace and spiritual gifts are turned to very
poisons.

If a man wants to avert this perfidious temptation, the will of God
must claim his submission as something other, something from outside. This otherness and differentness will be unmistakable where
God's demands say 'no' to a man's own will. That one side of the
divine which is at once so like and so utterly different from the
creature, that otherness that is specially meant for him alone, must
come into play before total likeness is realized in the authentic fulfilment of God's will; realized by the fact that man gives up his self-
seeking will and attains to his real will and real selfhood. That is only
possible when we encounter God's will through the intermediary of
another man: for only men are in the fullest sense *other*, more so than
things. Only other men have a will capable of opposing our own will.
Things do not will, they do not oppose. And man comes up against a
sheer impossibility when he tries to pit his will against their impertur-
ability. This impossibility he does understand and bows to the necessity
of it. But when someone who could will something else opposes him;
when someone could will as he wishes but does not do it, then a man
is up against foreign freedom, a freedom to resist, which makes any
coincidence with his own will impossible. Only when we meet the
will of God in the form of a commanding human will, are the attempts

of self-love to gain its ends by underhand methods doomed to failure. For it is not a perception of the necessity or the reasonableness of the command that is decisive in our response to it, but the freedom of the divine will which is its own ground and justification.

But if every human will is deflected from God by original sin and cramped up within itself, how is a man to interpret the will of God to another? He will try to make it serviceable to his own self-seeking ends, just like any other man; and the other's independence will rightly be affronted by this misuse of his obedience to God, whereby freedom is reduced to slavery. Only force and the fear of still greater discomfort can induce a man to make himself subject to another. And in actual fact, on the natural plane, graded relations between men, without which human society could not exist, are the expression of their various degrees of power and therefore entail, for the commanding party, a temptation to presumption and abuse, and for subordinates a provocation to insurrection and hatred. Only a man who incorporated the pure will of God as such and identified himself completely with it, would be safe from the risks involved. Only such a man, totally lacking in egoism, could be obeyed without reserve, without fear that he would offend true selfhood and personal dignity.

This man God gave mankind in the incarnation of Christ. In him humanity meets a Man attentive to the least stirring of his Father's will, the fulfilment of that will being as necessary to him as for the ordinary man food and drink (John 4. 34). Thus in all his ways and deeds and words it is God's will that encounters us, pure and unadulterated. Moreover this will comes to us as that of someone else: not as an unreliable flash of inspiration but as a clear command that may well say 'no' to our own proposals: which is a good means of testing authenticity in obedience to God.

An alien will, and yet for redeemed man living in grace, one not wholly nor absolutely foreign: for as God's will it has a kinship not to the sinful but to the restored ego of every Christian. In obedience to the revealed Word man does not submit to an utter stranger; such submission would be contrary to the nature and dignity of the person. What happens is that he finds himself, he finds his own deepest will, the will of the created creature and the child of God which can only agree with the Father's will. The will of Christ is thus the expression of the deepest, the redeemed being, of the Christian. And in this being God's will must therefore be findable. What redeemed individual being wants is none other than what Christ's word, coming from outside, also says. Thus it is in fact not alien, for all believers learn directly from God (John 6. 45).

But this state of correspondence is only possible to the redeemed and sanctified being of a Christian. So long as any of him is not redeemed, so long as egoism is still effective in him, he will find in his interior only perverse self-will, which even distorts and adulterates God's own messages to him. Whoever appeals to direct inspiration of the Holy Ghost against the revealed Word and its truth, allocates to himself very outstanding attributions: perfect freedom from all self-seeking, perfect sanctity; making claims that the saint would never make, because the saint knows very well how deeply man is implicated —having more intensely struggled against these pitfalls than other men. All enthusiasm and sectarianism based on personal inspiration are sheer self-deception and self-seduction, depriving piety of its true meaning, which is handing oneself over to God.

The word of God alone is the touchstone for the purity of our intentions. When they agree with it, then the danger of concealed perversity is removed. But it is with the *living* Word of God that man's intentions must coincide, a Word that may pull us up sharply and can put us straight when we go astray. This living Word is the living Christ and he alone, because he alone lives as God-Man by the fact of his union with the Father. The written word can also serve as touchstone. But it is not absolutely sufficient alone. The written word is capable of various interpretations and human perversity has seen to it that it is again and again interpreted in the most roundabout way. It has somehow to be made acceptable to given conditions of time and place, and this alone affords opportunities enough involuntarily to distort its true meaning under the promptings of self-love. It is not without deep significance that the Devil sought to turn Christ aside from his appointed way by quoting passages of Scripture. In his self-willed interpretation of God's word, man is actually listening to himself alone and not to God. This form of hidden disobedience is at times more harmful than open rebellion. The latter knows what it is about and cannot deceive itself irreparably under the appearance of doing good. But in private interpretation man maintains his own viewpoint with all the stubbornness and obstinacy that he ought to have put into fulfilling God's will. The Christ of the Bible and his words are also exposed to misrepresentation and a human account of the events described runs the risk of distorting God's will. If our Christ on whom we depend were only a past Christ, a Christ of whom the

Bible recounts a certain number of sayings and acts, as it does of other great men too, the whole effect of the incarnation would be frustrated.

But the Christ to whom we pray is far more than an historic figure because he is not only man. His manhood is caught up in the eternity and omnipotence of God. He lives in the midst of us in his Body the Church. Obedience to Christ thus becomes obedience to his Church as the propagator of God's word, as the living power of Christ alive in her. She utters this word in this or that form, as need may be, without distorting its meaning. In the will of the Church we come upon the will of Christ and the will of God, revealed as a will other than our own, but such that it corresponds to our own most individual, deepest will; for the Christian as member of the Church cannot ultimately want anything unconditionally apart from the will of God that reveals itself in this way.

The doctrines and rules of the Church give the Christian the lines to follow in his profession and indicate the spirit in which to make his decisions in particular cases. Within these lines he remains free to recognize in any given situation what God requires of him and to carry it out faithfully; and he will do both all the more perfectly the more deeply his redemption has penetrated into him. As already said, the given situation, even though conditioned by created causes, is in fact the work of God and thus a manifestation of his will, if it is considered in the light of faith and tackled in the power of faith.

To this situation must be reckoned the conditions of this graded society of ours, a gradation which facilitates human co-operation and promotes human culture. The fact that there are superiors and inferiors, rulers and ruled is inherent in the very nature of human affairs, and thus it is also the will of God (Rom. 13. 1 ff.). Christ too in his earthly life was subject to the authorities of the day, although as God's Son he might have been exempt (Matt. 17. 23–26). In fact all lawful authority is from God, and it is thus possible to see beyond the man issuing commands, to God himself, and to obey God himself in carrying out human commands. When this occurs, the alien nature of the command and the impersonality of the official are of no account, for God's will is not alien to his creatures.

Only Christ the Man-God can as Creator and Redeemer command a comprehensive obedience, from which nothing that is human is exempt. To him belongs the person as such, directly; his claims are addressed to the person and through the person they are relevant to all the various aspects of life. All earthly authority has its own field for immediate and direct action, for the purpose of ordering and directing life in common and work in common. The person as such is not directly subject to such authority, not on his own account, but only indirectly in relation to the special field of action. This accounts for the multiplicity of higher authorities. And it is this plurality alone that guarantees the maintenance of rightful freedom and independence and thus the dignity of the human person. Every earthly authority is of its very nature confined to a given field, and beyond this field it ceases to function as authority and ceases to represent God. And at this point obedience ceases too. And obedience also ceases, necessarily, when the demands of authority are in contradiction to the moral law and to revelation. The fact that a man has acted under orders may in given cases diminish his share of responsibility but it never entirely relieves him of it.

If some such infringement of the moral law is not involved, then, in his desire for conformity with Christ, for the sake of patient endurance with Christ when injustice is perpetrated, the Christian is free to obey even when authority transgresses its warrant. But the stipulation is that he must be the only one involved in this co-suffering. The situation changes immediately if his submission puts others in danger of having their freedom summarily curtailed. In such a case it is his duty to defend that freedom by resisting unwarranted impositions. And for this end he must be prepared to make sacrifices and even to face losing his job and missing opportunities for bettering himself, if sacrifice of this sort is in reasonable relation to the good he is out to defend. The duty to resist is the more pressing, the more influential a man's position is and the more the freedom of others depends on his attitude. Only through such resistance can greed for power and lust for domination be held in check and society be safeguarded from still greater calamities.

It is well known that the seduction of power is one of the most dangerous and insidious temptations of all; few others are so prone to swell to such monstrous proportions. More directly than any it impinges on God's rights. No man as mere man dare claim the unconditional and utter subordination of a fellow man. It is a crime worse than murder when right of freedom to think and act is suppressed and a tyrannical rule permits itself to prescribe to its subjects what they are to hold sacred, morally right, and true. For such exaction is not made upon man's bodily life which will in any case succumb to its mortality one day, but upon the very being of man intrinsically, and that is why it is so reprehensible.

Each single Christian must therefore endeavour in the spirit of Christ to recognize the will of God in any given situation and by faithful accomplishment of it to reduce self-love in himself. By such acts of loyalty he penetrates ever more deeply into Christ's mind and is thus enabled not only to come into correspondence with God's will, from case to case ever more purely and with less and less bias, but also in general behaviour to be more and more steadily at one with him, so that in place of his own perverse will the will of Christ shall more and more prevail. Thus the fulfilling of the will of God becomes more and more a matter of fulfilling his own will, in union through love with Christ. In this way freedom in obedience becomes a reality. The legalistic character of directives disappears by degrees. For in regard to one's own will a law is something imposed from outside, but when a rule is simply the expression of one's own intention, it would be acted upon even if it were not expressly there as a rule. Thus the law remains, and is nonetheless invalidated. It remains too, because here below man never attains to the condition of full life in Christ's spirit; and the less someone is actually Christian, the more stress has to be laid on the legalistic character of law. All other relaxations of the law, such as certain sects have adopted from time to time, lead to shocking moral aberrations.

So that is the life-work of each and every Christian: to bring his own will, down to its least stirrings, increasingly into correspondence with the will of God, and to let it be so light within him that he will see the way to find his own will in that correspondence. A sense of obligation arises from the very nature of the human will, as a thing created, but the deepest correspondence is only possible through love for Christ. Love achieves this miracle that two centres of personality harmonize perfectly, and without ceasing to be two, both live from one and the same hearth. Only love finds no difficulty in doing the will of the beloved as its own, even when its content is unclear, simply because the will of the beloved *is* its own. Only through love for Christ is it given us to live a human life straight from the heart of a divine Person and to love without self-deception. When Christ's mind is our own, we think like God himself. In this love obedience becomes perfect, and disappears to all intents and purposes, as the law does too. Thus St. Augustine is justified in saying, *Ama et fac quod vis*: you need only love, and then do as you will. For love wants only what the

beloved wants. Thus obedience ends in perfect love, even as it could
only begin in love. For already in the first act of submission something
of love, a beginning, a step up from the merely non-committal performance of a duty, must accompany it.

RELIGIOUS OBEDIENCE

So every Christian should conduct his life in Christ's spirit, in accordance with his revelation, and thus fulfil the will of God in all things.
But in ordinary Christian life there remains a fairly wide field where
revelation supplies no particular directives and where a Christian has
to think things over to discover the will of God. This is the field of
daily professional work and of many isolated instances where Christianity leaves it open to a man to decide this way or that. Here the same
temptation occurs that Christian endeavour encounters everywhere
else: to put our own will in the place of the divine will, to favour
ourselves in making our decisions, to preen ourselves indecently in our
successes and to be quite unduly cast down over misfortunes: taking
all our gifts and the circumstances of our existence for our private
property, for which we have only ourselves to thank. Our first inclination is always to be over-proud of our own achievements, proud of
the good we do, proud of our loyalty in God's service. Thus there is
always the danger that a subtle form of self-love will corrode even
Christian action and Christian endeavour. Once a man is aware of
how corruption threatens him on all sides, he can make up his mind—
not to resign his own power of choice, for that would mean ceasing
to be a person and would lead right away from perfection—but in the
field left open to him, to come to no decision on his own account, but to
give this right over to someone else, someone representing God's will,
and wholeheartedly to accept the decisions made for him. The danger
of a self-seeking view of the situation and of a self-seeking response to
its particular challenge is thus, as far as humanly possible, removed
once for all. A man's own will is so securely set within the will of God
that there is no chance left to it to boast of its own originality and its
capacity to make new discoveries and find applications for them.
Whatever is 'origin' is visibly and tangibly referred back directly to
God, who is alone pure origin in himself, and from whom every
created origin issues. This and nothing else is the meaning of Christian
obedience.

Such comprehensive obedience can and dare only be offered to a
man whose own will is, down to the smallest and most insignificant

details, wholly identified with the will of God. But this is true only of Christ; to him alone, the Holy One, is total obedience due (1 Peter 1. 14). But Christ is alive and present for every Christian in the Church. And such obedience is only permitted within the Church and as religious obedience. Now it is not within the Church's province to lay down detailed rules for Christian behaviour or to intervene in matters of choice, when this same Christian truth leaves a variety of possibilities open; and this is the usual position. The Christian has the right to decide without anyone making objections on religious grounds. But an obedience that extends to include the details of daily life offers within the sphere of the Church an even closer bond with Christ and a higher stage of discipleship.

Now, as we observed earlier, there have in every age been people in the Church who were possessed of Christ to an exceptional degree and who reflected his spirit even in apparently neutral matters and ordered them accordingly. If in the spirit of Christ a certain form of life based on imitation of Christ is adopted by a group of disciples and practised by them, then an Order springs up, and in this Order the same spirit will continue its work in the same outward form within the Church. In due course this way of life becomes established with its own customs, statutes and prescriptions—all with the purpose of keeping the original spirit alive.

Discipleship is essentially personal, and it therefore tends to a comprehensive ordering of life in the spirit of a person. But no one tradition and no one set of statutes can meet all possible cases at all given times. These are therefore supplemented by religious obedience to a superior, who with the consent of the Church represents the community of disciples. Through him the individual member of the community is enabled to shape his whole life in the spirit of the Order and thus bring it into conformity with Christ's spirit in all things. So within the Rule obedience embraces everything that is not wrong or contrary to the spirit of the Order. The superior is for his part bound to the Rule and to its spirit, and he sins against obedience when instead of following these he lets his own moods guide him and gives orders from egoistical motives.

Discipleship goes back through the master or founder to Christ himself, and religious obedience is not owed to the superior as the man he is, but through him to the founder of the Order and back to Christ himself. Here no more than in other cases where representatives are present is the inviolability of the direct approach to Christ and to God affected; everything depends on the spirit and intention in which the duty of obedience is paid. Here again that characteristic feature of Christianity is in evidence which we mentioned before: Christian worship is the worship of a wholly personal God, and all representation and mediation is done through persons in the first place, through a book in the second place, and finally through laws and rules. These constitute a framework outside which the discipleship incumbent upon all Christians (as laid down in the laws of the Church) or the special imitation of Christ characteristic of a given Order, can find no valid scope; or they lay down the lines along which matters can be settled which are indifferent in themselves, except that a certain conformity of behaviour may be necessary or desirable for practical reasons. But all such lesser matters deserve to be referred to Christ in intention; and obedience itself, inspired by love for him, will come alive as freely accepted submission to his person.

Only within this context is it comprehensible how one man can submit to another whose personal holiness is no sinecure against possible abuse. But as the powers of the man in authority are limited by statute, whatever the personal intentions of the superior may be the man under obedience has in the Rule an assurance that his obedience is relevant to his discipleship, deepening and vitalizing it.

To this the Order itself conduces, objectively. And the man under obedience can make his own contribution by the rightness of his attitude, acting according to God's will and not his own. The Church's sanction for the particular way of life chosen by an Order, and the Church's own guardianship of it, offer sufficient security that discipleship can be realized within it. Born of the sanctity of the founder, it cannot lead away from sanctity, and cannot bar the way to Christ for a man with a vocation. But where the special mission and the Church's sanction are lacking, obedience is not justified when it is extended to matters over which Christianity leaves the individual free to make his own choice, and above all it can never be unconditional.

Religious obedience so understood means an extension of the mystery of the Church and the Incarnation into the details of life. All religious obedience is of its very nature an extension of Christ's obedience to the Father, it means adopting the mind of Christ. By embracing this form of obedience a man renounces what lies nearest to him and is most individual to him: the right to dispose of himself; but he does it only in order to put this right back in God's hand through obedience. The man who is his superior is thus only an instrument and an occasion. The intention is directed through him to God. It is not to be denied that such obedience appears to natural human understanding as something quite insupportable. It is not as though it merely affected a man's exterior life, like ownership for instance, or even in a sense sexuality; here egoism is attacked in its inmost stronghold. And as natural man confuses self-seeking with selfhood itself—they are so inter-penetrated and practically inseparable after all—he has the impression that it is his very selfhood that he has renounced in renouncing egoism: obedience brings him face to face with a sort of spiritual death, the annihilation of individual freedom and the loss of human dignity. And all-embracing subjection to the will of another man appears all too humiliating. A man can take a pride in all other forms of renunciation, but with the renunciation that obedience requires of him it is not possible. And that is precisely what is intended.

The perfection of obedience consists, then, in accepting as one's own the will of God as revealed in the orders or requests of the superior. Some important claims are involved here. We always find lots of excuses for justifying a decision of our own making. We take no end of trouble to carry it out because that is how it is declared valid and our intelligence and skill are thus given publicity. Moreover we are ready to stand up for our decision against all comers. Obedience demands that we do just the same for the decisions of our superior and that we accept them and carry them out exactly as though they were our own. In fact we should actually identify ourselves with them as closely as though they were very deep decisions of our own, for it is at our deepest level that we want to place ourselves within the will of God. Compared to this depth of acceptance, the actual performance of the required act is not indifferent but it serves merely as a proof of the sincerity and steadfastness of our own personal acceptance of God's will.

So it is a matter of consequence that we should not ascribe any success to ourselves; after all we only want to do God's will and give him alone the credit for a success that is due not to ourselves but to him.

Thus and not otherwise is blind obedience. It is blind to its own recognition and to the pleasure normally provided by success, but far from blind to the success of the cause as willed by God. It is blind to personal advantage, but very much alive to God's advantage. And on that account it is never blind to the moral permissibility or otherwise of the demand made. For what is morally wrong cannot serve God's cause.

It is blind too in the sense that the qualities and faults of the man in authority have no positive weight, and when it comes to the decision to obey they are as it were non-existent. The man under obedience may see clearly that in view of practical results the order given is unintelligent or unwise. But he has no absolute interest in these practical results but only in God's will. And this can be effected through earthly failure; in fact best of all through failure, *vide* the Cross of Christ. This does not exclude the advisability of drawing the superior's attention to the true state of affairs when he appears to be on the wrong track, proposing other and better methods for carrying out his schemes. In fact in important matters it will be a man's duty to tell his superior what he thinks of the situation and what causes his misgivings; for the superior's intentions are not committed to certain methods, these are merely means to a desired end. His intention to reach this end includes the intention to discover appropriate methods for doing so, and it is quite in order to draw his attention to the possibility of better methods. There is of course a danger of incurring his dislike, or of being less well thought of or simply regarded as a nuisance. Such considerations should not however deter a man from doing his duty. If these were the reasons for remaining silent, then silence were no act of obedience: but an act done out of fear for the consequences, that is, out of cowardly self-interest.[1]

But if the superior, or in weighty matters the higher authorities in assembly, decide after consideration of the objection to remain by their original decision, obedience is due even when the result will be a fiasco.[2] A man knows then that beyond the will of his superior, God has something else in mind, and that he can make just as good use of the superior's error of judgement and lack of insight as of his human intelligence and practical sense. Thus obedience never requires that will and judgement should be given up, as is so often mistakenly sup-

[1] E. Mersch, *Morale et corps mystique*, 1949, 3rd edition: 'God who wants us whole does not begin by mutilating but by purifying. God who wants us active requires that we ourselves deploy our entire initiative in his service in dependence on his grace. Our expedients, our requests, our very protests, if the matter is worth while of course, are a part of the co-operation and an element of the obedience he requires of us. They may and in fact must be made, and an order can be resisted, but in a spirit of submission and with as pure a desire as possible to see God's will accomplished. An obedience that does not react may be a sign of frigidity in God's service, and perfection may exact that the last word but one should not be left to superiors.'

[2] H. Mogenet, *L'obéissance religieuse*, in *Revue d'Ascétique et de Mystique*, 27, 1951, p. 86: 'Our neighbour's egoism can only be conquered by goodness, and the momentary indocility towards God of a superior only by being ourselves docile.'

posed. Both should be all the stronger and clearer when they are released from the constricting effect of egoistical tendencies and motives and free to consider the situation as a whole. Self-love works like blinkers; it cuts a man off from certain aspects of reality and confines his sight to the small field of his own advancement, and in the long run its narrowness of vision becomes a real menace to his advancement. A man's own judgement, that unique view of the situation that every man possesses, ought to come into play, in all due proportion to the importance of the thing to be done; in fact it ought to be possible for him to tell his superior frankly and freely what his opinion is. The view of one man is always only a sectional view. It is the duty of a superior to inform himself as widely as possible of the true situation, by asking questions, basing his decision on the whole information available. Whereupon a man should give the whole strength of his mind to carry out the task appointed to him, growing in time so strong that he can overcome any contrary feelings. That is a good instance of how religious obedience means a broadening of vision conducive to unprejudiced understanding and the liberation and invigoration of the will.

However there is no denying that under the cover of obedience indolence and spiritual inertia can thrive and flourish. It may be pleasanter and easier to give orders to people who have relinquished all critical sense of their own and no longer possess a will. But that has nothing to do with the ideal of religious obedience. The lapse of authority into mere legality, firmly entrenched and exacting literal performance, is always, but particularly in religious life, an undignified distortion of true obedience. Inferiors and superiors are jointly responsible for the venture, if from different angles. It is after all the common venture of all concerned and each has his allotted part to play. And yet the man whose part it is to obey has so to identify himself with what is required of him that it could have been his own idea. If he fails out of fear or time-serving to make his scruples known, he is letting himself down just as much as when he makes difficulties through a propensity to grouse or out of vanity or sheer contrariness: things which presumably have nothing to do with the matter at issue, but have a great deal to do with his own self-love.

The superior is just as much committed to obedience as the rest. He is no less under obedience than they are, and this not merely in the sense that, apart from the Pope, every superior has a superior of his own; but actually as superior. For his position as superior can have no meaning except to do God's will. He too must try to get rid of egoism in order to recognize God's will more and more clearly as indicated by circumstances. He must not allow his position to become an opportunity for getting his own way and making the most of himself. He dare not give orders merely in order to make his subordinates feel his heavy hand—a temptation to which weak and inwardly insecure people are very liable to succumb.

Abuse of authority provokes a subordinate to take up a refractory attitude for which the superior is part-responsible. Admitting how one-sided and limited any human view of reality is, the superior dare not reject the help of counsel other than his own, for every situation is the clearer for being seen through more than one pair of eyes. Just as it may be incumbent on a man to draw his superior's attention to some apparent error of judgement, for the same reason the superior is more or less bound to lend an attentive ear to the advice given him, in all due proportion to the importance of the matter under consideration, and to act on it if need be. Nonetheless the decision remains truly and wholly his own and he must bear full responsibility for what comes of it, particularly where no success is registered.

The position of superior is not supposed to make life easier and more comfortable for him. He should of course avoid taking on lesser jobs that might hamper him in performing his special function. But his position is no sinecure for comfort. He has to see to it that he is not waited upon more than strictly necessary, and he has to take care not to let his office be an opportunity for exerting authority for its own sake. The tokens of respect due to the office will be accepted, and if necessary exacted, but only as due to the office, not the man. He and those who serve under him have one and the same duty: service to the cause in all selflessness (Matt. 20. 25 ff.; Mark 10. 42; Luke 22. 25). Moreover he is bound to it to the same degree of commitment, if in other ways. The more a man has, in obedience, laid all responsibility for his own personal concerns in the hands of his superior, so that thinking about them can no longer be a veil and a cover for egoism, the greater is the obligation of the superior to care for each and every one of his sons in God with all the keenness and devotion that a man might give to his own affairs. As representative of the divine will he will endow his office with something of the fatherly love of God who sees to it that each man has his due. He is not there to lord it over those he has charge of, they are not his slaves (1 Peter 5. 2 ff.); all together serve God as fellow workers in the cause of Christ.

Thus the deeper meaning of obedience gradually comes to light; it should create a sense of community in which through love for Christ's cause and through work in common, love of fellow men will spring to life too, its expression being community of judgement and action.[1] The ideal state of affairs would be one where a community was so strongly possessed of the same spirit in Christ that unity of views and resolutions would be spontaneous. But the limitations of the human mind and the multiplicity of points of view make it impossible for this fundamental unity to suffice when decisions on practical matters are at stake. One man must be entrusted with the duty of making decisions. Love of God will make obedience and acceptance easier to the rest; and just as though each one of them had of his own accord come to the decision made by authority, its performance is the common concern of all. But to God alone is due the merit for the decision itself and for its successful issue. As long as a man remains proud of his own performance—and who dare say he is no longer proud?—he is still not clear in his mind as to the connection between first and finite causes. The first cause does not however displace secondary causes, as though pride in his own achievement could take away from God's glory. God does not need renown in the human sense. But when a man seeks even a secret self-satisfaction in his own successes, he is failing to recognize God as what He is, He from whom are derived all being and all causality of creatures; he presumes he is somehow something on his own and in a position to act accordingly, apart from God. But a man who knows the truth no longer refers to himself as final deciding centre, but to God. Then he has no particular interest in being known as the originator of a scheme and being honoured for it. His only concern is that the cause be served, and the only cause in all causes is the will of God.

By adopting this attitude a man gets the better of envy, which is not so much concerned in doing the right thing as in seeing that it is done by me and no one else. It is not the renown of his name that a man's works are to proclaim: that is not the hallmark they should bear for all to see; the glory of God the eternal is all their praise. Thus obedience implies a share in the good works done by others, even when what is done is felt to be personally injurious, as St. Paul tells us: 'Some . . . are moved by party spirit, proclaiming Christ from wrong motives, just because they hope to make my chains gall me worse. What matter, so long as either way, for

[1] St. Thomas, *St.Th.*, 1a, 2ae, Q. 99, a.1 ad 2.

private ends or in all honesty, Christ is proclaimed? Of that I am
glad . . .' (Phil. 1. 7 f.).

This state of mind means death to the presumptuous lesser ego. But
it is a source of strength and peace, particularly in difficult and hazar-
dous enterprises. Any man acquainted with the multiple modes of
human feelings would never desire to hold office as superior, did he not
know that earthly success or failure is ultimately no human matter.
Indeed we do not even know if we have the right so to describe any
occurrence, so little can we foresee the further consequences of our
interventions in the world, let alone suppose we hold the strings. A
human decision is always one among many final causes which contribute to the shaping of an event. The larger it looms and the more
powerfully, the more it escapes prediction and human piloting.
Between the idea and the reality—Between the motion and the act—
Falls the Shadow.[1] That is why planning and what comes of it are
always so far apart. It often happens in life that thankless tasks have to
be taken on and faithfully performed, when on the earthly level anything but success can be awaited. The knowledge that the essential success of the procedure shall never be put in question by outward appearances gives strength and courage in these difficult situations. In faith
man knows that what is required of him is not success—people may
expect it, God does not—but that he do what he has to do.

And no more than that is required of superiors. Thus, they should not
let pride or fear drive them to do everything themselves in order to
anticipate any need for decision by others. They should not let an
unreasonable number of small detailed prescriptions stifle all joy in
work.[2] And if the essence of obedience is always the same, its outward
form changes, and the range of what needs detailed ordering and what
only needs setting on the right lines changes, not only with the nature
of every new undertaking but also with time and place. The more
independent the average man is, at a given period or at a certain social
level, the less is it necessary to exact implicit obedience on every point,

---

[1] T. S. Eliot, *The hollow men.*

[2] H. Mogenet, *ibid.*, p. 84: 'Such authority can have a degrading effect. A *Sulpicien*
prudently referred to this in an answer to the *Jeunesse de l'Eglise* enquiry: *Le Christianisme
a-t-il dévirilisé l'homme?* . . . "In practice, we have to admit that we have more often
been summoned to obey blindly than to collaborate. In certain religious houses in particular, the adage: 'to see God in the Superior' is understood in a sense which leaves no room
at all for conscious collaboration. And indeed a great many minds are wounded by it
and react; and then they either give in or run riot. And behind the literalness of meticu-
lous, frightened obedience appear a critical spirit and a desire to get round the rule which
make this obedience look despicable." '

so long as the right spirit predominates. No man can take the place of God's providence. When to the best of his knowledge and conscience a man has tried to do what he believed to be required of him at the time, after giving the matter due consideration, and above all, taking the trouble to do justice to it, quite unselfishly, he really has done all that can be required of him. The rest lies in the hand of God, for whom the ignorance, dullness and weakness of his creature are tools just as serviceable as his all too short-sighted wisdom and his so-called strength. God always attains his end, for he holds all causes in his hand and every least flicker of life in them is his.

HONOUR AND RENOWN BEFORE GOD

Thus, in spite of all appearances to the contrary, obedience brings a man face to face with God. It frees him to serve the cause itself and concentrates all his powers on it. Labouring in transiency and uncertainty, it is the imperishable that he is realizing with the infallible pledge of true success. Man cannot live without feeling he is granted some sort of acknowledgement. For his is no mere isolated life here, lived for himself alone, but he is created to share his life with his fellows. Acknowledgement from his fellows gives him strength and self-confidence. But here too, since the Fall, his questing has taken the wrong direction and focused on lesser and more exterior things; whereas acknowledgement is ultimately a matter between himself and God. God's approval should be sufficient to him and he should live to please God and God alone. But since God's approval or otherwise is no longer directly known to him, in his craving for acknowledgement he has turned to creatures, vainly seeking in outward honours and titles a stability they have not got it in them to provide.

Fame and success here on earth: those were the gifts man sought from his idols, mistaking them for signs of divine power. And here too the revelation of Christ went counter to natural religious feeling. Christ did not appear as the highly renowned ruler and sovereign of the world, nor as a universally acclaimed and revered man of wisdom and learning. Indeed the greater part of his life was spent in obscurity in Nazareth, and in small country towns of no particular note he worked at an ordinary trade to earn his living. Of this stage in his story the evangelist merely tells us that he was subject to his parents (Luke 2. 51). Is it not incomprehensible waste, sheer folly, that he, the Son of God, who had so much to tell the world, spent his whole life up to his thirtieth year working as a carpenter? His preaching and teaching only

lasted for a short time, and it was mostly done among the people of
Galilee rather than the learned men of Jerusalem, he preached in disparaged Jewry rather than at the headquarters of world government
and worldly wisdom. Was not the greater part of his precious life as
good as thrown away—in fact irretrievably lost?

Now, in Jesus' life nothing is accidental and everything is significant
as revealing God at work. We have here a revelation of the nature of
God which it is hard for man to grasp. True, all glory and honour and
power are due to God (Apoc. 4. 11; 5. 12 ff.). But he does not need
them. He does not need his creature and his creature's acclaim and
acknowledgement in order to be God. For he has all the acknowledgement he needs within himself, in the unity in love of the three Divine
Persons, of which each with the whole eternal power of God's Being
desires, acknowledges and affirms the other, unceasingly and ever-
lastingly. This inconceivable, incomprehensible independence of what
his creatures may think of him appeared in Christ's human life as utter
detachment from honours and renown, as disregard of misrepresentation, with a complete lack of pretension finally collapsing into sheer
catastrophe: and this was a display of true honour and renown as
seen by God (Rom. 4. 2). It was independent of all human judgement,
and what was the judgement of sinful man worth—man separated
from God (John 8. 21–47)?

For a creature there is no true honour other than the honour of
God. God's judgement alone is valid, it alone is decisive. In him alone
is reflected man's true worth. To be is to be acknowledged by God
and confirmed by him. Christ had no other concern but God's judgement. And his lowly life in Nazareth is a provocation and a contradiction to men's judgement designed to compel them to consider what it is
that gives human activity a value. It is before God's judgement that
man's obedience stands or falls, so that however glorious and successful
his deeds may appear to be, he will see they are nothing when they
cannot stand before God; whereas the most lowly act possesses eternal
value when it is done for the sake of conforming to God's will. Thus
obedience lends new dignity and incalculable efficacy to every least
human action. The quiet working days in Nazareth were not lost to
the world. If today manual labour is no longer disparaged in the way it
was in heathendom, and human dignity is known to include the dignity
of the working man, it is but the continuation of the revolutionary act
begun in Nazareth. Nowadays no work is too low or too humble to
have a significance of its own. No life is so irretrievably meaningless

and humdrum that it can no longer be productive of eternal values.

Christian obedience delivers a man from the urge to be of importance to his fellows, an urge that can wrack him without ever bringing him satisfaction. Full acknowledgement by our fellows can never be the aim of our life, as Hegel supposed. To begin with, it is an impossibility. First of all there is egoism in the way, driving each man on to better himself at the cost of his neighbour, and keeping him so exclusively concentrated on himself and his own wishes and fears that he is no longer capable of being truly on the spot. To be completely present is a state that is in any case debarred by the body, for its natural inertia and inelasticity always stand in the way of the complete union of two people in their innermost heart of hearts. It means that one person's standpoint can never exactly be the standpoint of another, so that self-knowledge and knowledge of another remain quite different things and never entirely coincide.[1]

Thus man is ultimately alone; human renown stops short of this point, and no title or outward rank can alter a man's position as it is in reality. If here there is emptiness, no amount of recognition from fellow men can fill it. If a man is conscious of his nothingness, titles and insignia will not raise him into being. And he knows it. Hence the insatiability of his greed for honours, of his pride, of his vanity, and the deceptiveness of all of them. In the depths of his being man is only what he is before God. Human judgement has no validity at this point, it cannot even reach it. There is a final field where a man stands alone when he does not stand in God. No power can force its way in. Human love itself cannot get past the final barrier and turn solitude into company, unless by bringing love of God in with it. As no one has his being from another man, and as all being springs from God's creative act alone, no creature has admission to the core and base of this being except through God and in God, and that will only be possible when the body has ceased to be an obstacle through transfiguration.

It is in vain that fallen man seeks to overcome his solitude by turning to other creatures. When disillusionment finally comes upon him, he locks himself up in icy pride and feels bitter disdain for his fellows—and if he is a great man, he will do so all the more. Obedience shows the way to gain God's acknowledgement, which is the only acknowledgement that is valid, giving a man rest for his soul and firm ground

[1] Cf. J.-P. Sartre, *L'être et le néant*, Part 3.

under his feet, not to be shaken by failure and apparent miscarriage of hopes and plans.

Turning to God resolves the inmost and most solitary solitude and releases from the craving for human approval. The truth of the words becomes apparent: 'A man must be content to receive the gift which is given him from heaven, and nothing more' (John 3. 27). The number of talents he receives does not depend on him and he will not be called to account on that score. Awareness of this fact allays jealousy and envy and makes a man capable, at last, of recognizing his fellow men, and by doing so helping them to improve their performance. Consequent on this Christian state of mind are a new independence from men's judgements coupled with a new friendliness of approach to other people. As ever, only the supernatural can set men free, even in the natural sphere.

FROM FEAR TO FREEDOM

Ultimately, the scope of obedience in faith widens out till it includes everything that happens. But it all comes about through God's co-operation alone. God is in it all, working for the good of his own (Rom. 8. 28), whatever the intentions of men may be—those whom he uses to carry out his purposes. Therefore the obedient man will be one who seeks to see the power and love of God at work in all occurrences, just as in the spirit of poverty he restores to the good things of this world their fundamental character as creatures created by God. In obedience proper, as in all else, man's gaze should be directed through finite causes to God, for God it is who gives finite causes their causality as well as their being, and works out his purposes through them, whatever they may do. Superficially seen, events are more often menacing and distressing than cheerful and encouraging. This is no accident, it is inherent in the fundamental character of life in this world, and in particular of human life. Biological life is of its nature destined to die, and this exposes it to perpetual menace and suffering. An animal knows nothing about it and suffers pain only momentarily. Mortality and suffering only become sharply painful in man, because of the way his spirit is bound to his body, suffering with it and in it, and on the surface feels itself threatened in its existence too. But as spirit it extends out beyond this menaced condition. To enter freely into misfortune or disaster is its prerogative. Its fate is in its hands. But this is a form of security that cannot be perceived, and thus explicit consciousness finds it to be non-existent. Nonetheless faith assures man of the existence of security at the base of being in the creative love of God; but reminds him that what is of the earth cannot be taken under cover of this security without painful transformation. The only beloved Son of God had to undergo death on the Cross to enter into the glory of the resurrection, because that was the way of suffering by which alone his brethren could be brought to perfection (Luke 24. 26; Heb. 2. 10 ff.).

Whoever in the spirit of obedience has grown accustomed to see God in all things and to live with him in a grace-given intimacy, has an impregnable core to his being that the onslaught of earthly powers will nevermore be able to shatter. No threat and no torment can frighten him into wavering in the fulfilment of his duty. External success and failure are divested of their disproportion. They are not matter for indifference, but they are no longer final. Thus success ceases to fascinate and dazzle, only to cast a man into the abyss. And failure no longer shakes that deep confidence of his, the loss of which can make a man hurl himself to the ground in impotent despair. The characteristic feature of human existence, that growing to 'perfect manhood, that maturity which is proportioned to the completed growth of Christ' (Eph. 4. 13), will when good will is present most certainly be realized through God's grace.

To gaze upon human history without the light of faith is to gain a totally wrong impression of human achievement, unless a man prefer to close his eyes to the terrible spectacle and live on wishful dreams. How unstable everything is that man has done. How rapidly the greatest powers fall to ruin. How inconclusive the findings of philosophy remain. How impotent technical inventions are in the face of real need. How much even the very best is liable to abuse through stupidity or wickedness. And if this is true of man's greater works, then what significance can the life and efforts of other men have, countless and uncountable, who disappear leaving no trace of their existence, and yet have to suffer too. In the face of all this, how can one speak of the dignity and worth of every single human life?

Faith however shows us in Christ's life the true meaning of all earthly activity. This activity is only at home in this world and can only leave its mark on things and conditions here. Every act of withdrawal into a purely interior life reduces a man in stature and is in any case only partially realizable. Nevertheless, whatever man does has a meaning beyond the immediate occasion, with a direct reference to an ultimate meaning. This is no other than the formation of Christian personality. The realization of this eternal meaning is bound to no particular external circumstances, but depends simply on the freely adopted attitude of the individual and his own human efforts. In the face of this fact, the position a man may attain to in the world has no ultimate validity but is merely a temporal and secondary matter. The ultimate meaning of life, which is everybody's concern, sets every human countenance alight with an unearthly light only to be approached with reverential awe. But for such over-tones, no humanism could survive.

What Christian obedience calls for is not indifference to the duties life imposes on us; still less is it an excuse for carelessness or indolence in performance. No, what are called for are self-surrender and freedom —both: that is why Christian obedience is so difficult to carry out properly. A Christian has to apply himself to the performance of current duties with just the amount of industry due to them, just the right expenditure of energy having regard to the job as a whole. As far as it depends on him, he leaves nothing undone that could contribute to the success of the venture. And yet he may not lose himself in it. He has his final freedom and independence to safeguard, not only in his attitude to possible success but even in his attitude to the progress of his work. For ultimately he is not doing the job for its own sake, here and now alone; that is a penultimate point of view. But he actually intends it as a means by which to fulfil God's will, which is the only thing a creature of God can desire unconditionally and enter upon with profoundest devotion and self-sacrifice. It is precisely this will of God's that challenges all a man's keenness and energy, but by its own methods, with none of the usual risk of entanglements, no fear that he will become so passionately engrossed that he can no longer extract himself when God calls him to leave it and move on, no fear of his becoming a prey to those heart-rending regrets for the past that are so prejudicial to work in a new field. Keenness comes easily to a man, so does detachment—as separate states of mind. Difficulties occur when red-hot zeal and utter interior freedom have to be combined. Only a man who has found his ultimate absolute base can run to utter devotion without getting lost. The real meaning of any historical moment is beyond history, beyond this world. Events succeed one another and are gone, leaving as residue monuments that endure for a time, only to perish in due course. They are sealed with no inherent assurance of permanency; so long as they last, they serve as enrichment and increase for human life. They are gifts which may be accepted in grateful piety, qualities calling for appreciation; their beauty awakens joy, but they are not there to distract a man from his true vocation. Here too he remains free, not because he has too little understanding or too much detachment, but he has still greater things in mind and at heart. Moreover though the world glower upon him as it is wont to do, it will not unnerve him or drive him to the brink of despair. He has no need to steer clear of either joy or sorrow for fear of drowning in their sheer immensity. Nor need he turn his back on reality in stoical indifference. Without marked stress or strain he can remain quiet and composed amid the whirlwind of events, squarely set on such firm and deep interior foundations that he no longer has to seek the support of any transient thing, a thing that may itself give way and let him down. Life's riot of complexity all points but one way for him: to do God's will, more and more careless of whatever earthly consequences he may encounter. With this innermost conviction of faith a man will gladly echo the words of the Apostle: 'Who can be our adversary, if God is on our side? He did not even spare his own Son, but gave him up for us all; and must not that gift be accompanied by the gift of all else? Who will come forward to accuse God's elect, when God acquits us? Who will pass sentence against us, when Jesus Christ, who died, nay, has risen again, and sits at the right hand of God, is pleading for us? Who will separate us from the love of Christ? Will affliction, or distress, or persecution, or hunger, or nakedness, or peril, or the sword? For thy sake, says the scripture, we face death at every moment, reckoned no better than sheep marked down for slaughter. Yet in all this we are conquerors, through him who has granted us his love. Of this I am fully persuaded; neither death nor life, nor angels or principalities or powers, neither what is present nor what is to come, no force whatever, neither the height above us nor the depth beneath us, nor any other created thing, will be able to separate us from the love of God, which comes to us in Christ Jesus our Lord' (Rom. 8. 31–39).

So in the end obedience leads to real security and true freedom, the freedom Christ has won for us (Gal. 4. 31; 5. 1), after it had appeared that he was depriving us of all security and delivering us over to submit meekly to the wanton action of others. On the worldly plane it may indeed be so. But the world itself can only offer penultimate securities which give way in course of time, and it makes very little real difference, whether their withdrawal occurs at once or later. In the love of God, imperceptibly and only apprehensible to faith, there grows within a man a haven of security which never fails him and which will one day come into its own, when transfiguration takes place.

Thus religious obedience is genuine liberation from the shackles of fear. Its focus is beyond the threat of harm and it lets a man live for that vista. Except when acting in the spirit of faith, a man reacts out of fear and he is not completely free however much he may believe the contrary. He cannot do good when it makes him fear for consequences unfavourable to his immediate interests. Indeed fear often hinders him from even seeing what good is there to be done. The right opportunities appear still-born and improbable. Only the man who is free has an eye open for all sorts of possibilities and is not to be held back by any bugbear in the world from setting to work on the best of them. The best, however, is always what corresponds to God's will here and now.

In utter devotion to the eternal will of God, man accomplishes the impossible, he gathers up all that is merely factual and accidental in his life and the circumstances of it, and sweeps it into the scope of his freedom. Indeed the very factuality of human life is due to the pure freedom of God and is thus reflected back on to the creature. Whatever it may consist in, a product of freedom cannot simply be dismissed as predetermined. Indeed it might well have been other, had freedom wished it so. So it is that factuality makes manifest the essentially creaturely nature of human life: it is nothing of itself and is thus certainly not the basis of its own being; but no more is it just a link in an impersonal predetermined chain of events, a condition which man might have found reassuring; but no, a personal will, a free will called man into being, and thus he stands responsible before this will. Fear is, at bottom, fear of the unknown, which is in reality God.

But when, united to Christ, man places himself obediently within this creative will of God, and consents to it as alone decisive, then he comes right on to the base of his own existence and recognizes it as freedom; not arbitrary freedom but the freedom of everlasting love. And now he sets to work in loving communion to fulfil this creative will which is also the basis of his own existence—with all its sundry dispositions.

Those things that so easily give rise to grudges and resentment— things about man's life that are so hard to understand and account for: accidents of birth and rank, wealth and intellectual endowment, difficulties encountered and undeserved failures—all can now be accepted, for in the loving will of God a man is now part-author of them in their origin, and this gives them a special significance of their own. Indeed the significance lies in the act of acceptance itself: in facts accepted as they are because thus God will be acknowledged in the unconditional freedom of his plans and actions; God will be accepted as God. In a world which has the personal freedom of everlasting God at its origin, a purely factual standpoint goes so far and no farther.

But a man who only wants to do good, if possible simply for the sake of doing good, is active at the very source and springhead of God's primacy, and God acts only in the unconditional freedom of love. Such a man's actions spring from the depth of his own being, from the point where it is touched by the creative hand of God. Earthly man is in a continual state of being driven—even when he believes he is acting freely. Greed and fear, the desire for possessions, pleasure, power and consideration, together with fear of suffering and disgrace, lash him on and condition him far more than he conditions himself. Under their influence a man remains alien to himself. Only one who acts straight from the true source is himself in his act and has a firm stance because he is anchored in God. That is how, with the most trifling means, the saints of history attained to the highest and noblest ends, the most spiritual ends of all. It is precisely the people whose mind is not all set on having their names remembered by posterity when they produce creative works, who have most successfully struck out on new ventures. For they harkened only to the call of the hour in which God's will was made apparent.

In this they resemble their Lord and Master Jesus Christ. His life was not spent in having everything his own way (Rom. 15. 3), building up his reputation and making a show of himself. He wanted nothing but his Father's will, he sought only the Father's glory and he was consumed in this will. St. John's Gospel is the one which gives the most revealing account of his divine and human greatness, stressing most markedly his obedience, a sense of dependence that extended down to the least things of all.

Over his whole mission there lies this intention of obedience to the Father: 'It is the will of him who sent me, not my own will, that I have come down from heaven to do' (John 6. 38). 'It was from God I took my origin, from him I have come' (8. 42; 7. 29). All his thoughts and judgements and acts were co-ordinated to the Father's will, down to the smallest detail. 'The Son cannot do anything of his own pleasure, he can only do what he sees his Father doing; what the Father does is what the Son does in his turn. The Father loves the Son, and discloses to him all that he himself does. And he has greater doings yet to disclose to him, for your astonishment' (John 5. 19). 'I cannot do anything on my own authority; I decide as I am bidden to decide, and my decision is never unjust, because I am consulting the will of him who sent me, not my own' (5. 30). Even what he teaches is not his own: 'The learning I impart is not my own, it comes from him who has sent me' (7. 16). He did not choose his circumstances nor his own fellow workers, but accepted those whom the Father had entrusted to him, chosen out of the world (John 17. 6). Indeed he laid down his life of his own accord, because that is the charge the Father had given him and he could reveal his love to him by carrying it out (John 10. 17). Dependence on his Father infuses every detail of his life. He let Lazarus die and laid himself open to the accusation of being coldly indifferent to the sufferings of his friends, or of not being able to help them more than anyone else could do. Only when the time appointed by his Father had come did he set out on his way to Bethany and performed his great miracle (11. 1 ff.). He did not look to his reputation (8. 50), but sought the glory of the Father. 'What I do is always what pleases him' (8. 19). That is the content and meaning of his life. To do the Father's will was as urgently necessary to him as food and drink are for the natural man (4. 34).

But no one would try to make out that this all-embracing obedience to the Father was derogatory to Christ's personality and diminished it in any way. In all the history of the world there is no man so great, powerful and commanding as he; no one has more continuously and profoundly influenced the course of history than he did through his so short term of work; no one else achieved so much with such a minimum of earthly means, purely from the power of his own personality. So it is therefore not derogatory to true selfhood when a man's attitude to the source of all selfhood and all originality is one of implicit obedience uniting him to this source, and God's pure primacy lays hold on him and streams out into the world through him.

Church history proves it. The saints who knew nothing outside God's will as it was made plain to them through human means, are after Christ the strongest and most unique personalities of all. Statesmen and commanders are nothing in comparison, nor are they successful in introducing new ideas and stimulating new attitudes to reanimate hearts and minds. The saints are the great revolutionaries. But theirs were bloodless revolutions, they did not sacrifice men to false ideals, nor did they found movements with the power-lust as their basis and an urge to dominate that knew no bounds. The changes they brought about are changes for the better, making men happier and more inclined to goodness, and providing opportunities for new inner freedom. The saints could do it because they were completely ready for the call of the hour in which the will of God was made known to them. They stood for their cause, not for themselves. And thus no humiliation could make them waver, no calamity could daunt them. They knew that the power of God was on their side. Their humility prevented them from becoming bogged in mere human obstinacy, on the other hand in the hour of trial and misrepresentation it was their safeguard from loss of courage and the onset of despair.

For such hours were not spared any of them. All had to go through the valley of death where failure, misrepresentation, persecution and shipwreck were the order of the day. For it was only by facing this terrible night that they could be cleansed of that trace of egoism which, when everything else is given up, still leaves a man all too ready to take pride in his own achievements. After all, success is no sign of election or pledge of salvation, least of all financial success. Once all dross was burnt away and melted away in those scorching furnaces, once only the pure gold of selfless love remained, then the power of God could make use of his saints to influence the world without any risk of being deflected from its end or misused by egoism. Set at the heart of Christ's love, in his name they radiated out into the world that power of love of God's, a power which does not outwardly alter men and conditions, but settles in that innermost core of man which is the centre of what he knows as the world.

Hence the real effect of the saints is similar to that of the power of God, in that it does not focus on this or that particular point but is destined to transform the world from its source of origin outwards. In due course the power issuing from this new centre disperses through the different ranges of life, moulding them from within to concur with the spirit within them. This we can observe in history; Christianity was introduced neither as a cultural reform nor as a political or economic reform. And yet its influence in all those spheres has been revolutionary; and we are not at the end of it yet.

So religious obedience means not a diminishing but an enhancing of true personality, union with the absolute personal being of God through surrender to Christ the man, whose Humanity was that of no independent human person but wholly that of the Word. Obedience means being set free to live continually on the alert for what alone has reality and duration, the will of God. Only in so far as human action runs along with this will can it share its creative power. Obedience points to the spiritual power which alone is origin and which would readily bring its weight to bear on all phenomena. Obedience is a release from the pressure and compulsion exercised by outward conditions and situations; merely by exerting his own will, man has not got it in him to do much, if anything at all, to produce circumstances or to alter them. But now they lose their rigidity, now, fluid and flexible, they become vessels for the inpouring of the spirit, without any change in their appearance. But in relation to God's action the world possesses no durable consistency of its own to offer God as a field for it, but is simply what he wishes and what he intends, for without God's will it is nothing; in just the same way, invisibly but effectively, human circumstances are flexible to obedience and capable of modulation; their rigidity relaxes and becomes amenable. And that is what the spiritualization of the world means: not a pantheistic process by which matter is merged into an impersonal spiritual substance, of which it was supposed to have been a manifestation, not in the foundering of everything into an indeterminate impersonal unity, but in the flooding of those cramped, tight places at the lower levels of life by an overwhelming force which is none other than the power of the spirit itself, so that service done on behalf of the spirit be whole-hearted.

Thus in the sphere of action with its base in selfhood, obedience works to the same end as poverty in regard to things, and chastity in regard to life: that is, it effects permanent and lasting transformation. Man becomes all agog for what is real and authentic. He gives himself over to God and wants no other base, and now he can dare to go abroad into the menaced fields of his earthly existence with all their would-be precious adjuncts. He knows that in this mobility, this lunge outwards into the void, his most individual self, that which is really himself is not endangered—far from it: it is real life at last, life according to the laws of the spirit. For spirit is mobility, it is origin and originality. Its mobility is not the pain-ridden mobility of matter nor is its originality anything to do with the so-called novelties of the busy world which leave everything as it was, *ad nauseam*. But we have here a constant of mobility issuing from its own origin and its own freedom, sharing in the creative originality of God which never grows old or stale.

It is therefore no accident that the images Holy Scripture uses to describe the Holy Spirit all point to those qualities of mobility and lightness inseparable from a constant of irresistible power and strength. The winged mobility of the dove, in the power of the spirit hovering without visible support or darting hither and thither (Matt. 3. 16; Mark 1. 10; Luke 3. 22); the wind, of which no one knows the way it came or the way it goes (John 3. 8), which no one can grasp and hold for it is like nothing in a man's hand and yet is capable of rooting up great trees and lashing the sea into mighty billows and destroying men's handiwork: the wind that also blows so soft and cool that life can take a deep reviving breath of it. The spirit is fire (Acts 2. 3), the flame that springs up to burn away all impurity and itself remains unsullied. The elusive wavering flame that sets all things aglow and transforms them into its own brightness, which warms too and dispenses life—like wind a Nothing, full of irresistible power. It is running water too (John 7, 38), helpless and shapeless, compelled to take on alien forms; and yet nothing can resist it, rocks and mountains give way to its quiet persistent action. And when it comes to the right soil, it produces life and fertility. The lightness and ductility that look like impotence and are in reality the hallmark of superior strength sure of itself and free, are also symbolized in oil, which keeps things supple and prevents friction; oil that nourishes and heals. Obedience brings a man right within the divine life of the Spirit. Here he learns where true power lies. He sees that earthly power with its heavy hand and oppressive ways, its abuse of force, its prisons, armoured cars and armoured ships, is no true power. It is far too unwieldy and torpid. Nor is heavy gold, for all its glint and purchasing power, true power; for this, as Simon the Sorcerer had to admit (Acts 8. 12), cannot be bought. Its sheer unwieldy ponderousness, functioning thus and not otherwise, is a sign of the inherent weakness of power based on matter. It is a power that has no power over itself, a power without controls, that is, no power at all in the real and true sense. Of itself it can only act destructively, it can only annihilate. It becomes creative only when it enters the service of a good spiritual power and is transformed into an instrument for good. To accept this good and true power, foster it, become permeable to it so that it will beam out into the world in all we do, that is the earthly significance of obedience. However contradictory it may sound, obedience exists for the sake of freedom; and obedience is genuine when it springs from the spiritual freedom of him who obeys.

The part religious obedience can play in the relations of people to one another is now plain. Human society cannot get along unless it is very variously graded. This is not only due to the ineradicable inequality of people among one another, which need only be forcibly levelled out for a time to make itself all the more apparent. There is also the fact that for a number of people to work together effectively, some sort of order is essential. As civilization becomes more complicated, the degrees and kinds of group work increase and multiply. Here two fundamentally different attitudes exist, though hardly apparent as such in ordinary life. Unredeemed man likes to assert himself and make use of other people, willy-nilly. Power is in the hands of economists and politicians, or else of men of brawn. Good sense would have such power held in check, but a subordinate knows it as a menace and is made to feel its full weight the moment he attempts to break away from his subordinate state. So he remains where he is, in many cases grudgingly, looking out for chances to retaliate on others. Even if he submits without a murmur, he is queasily aware that complaints would remain unheard anyhow. This is degrading and offensive to his individuality and his personal dignity. He loses his self-respect and becomes a slave in his own view; going about with a sense of injury. And to be rid of it he pretends to like his impotence and to approve of it. Meanwhile his chief has things all his own way and comes up against his neighbour's fence as his first obstacle: his own freedom imposes no constraint on him. His derogatory attitude to his slaves and the hollowness of his self-centred life cause him to lose all respect for the human person as such and turn him into a tyrant, base, profoundly discontented and chronically raging. It is no matter of chance that all unmitigated rule so soon degenerates and perpetrates atrocities. If there remains an element of luck in who reaches the top, such a state of affairs never produced anything but arbitrary acts and abuse of authority. But bloody revolutions do nothing to improve conditions that are *per se* below the human level. They merely replace one set of tyrants and victims by another; the disorder remains the same.

Quite rightly, everyone agrees that no one has the right to lord it over him, to give orders off his own bat and command obedience; no one has the right to reduce others to a state of abject dependence simply and solely because he happens to be in a better position to do so. Everyone is free as a person, everyone is called to decide for himself, and everyone is exempt from being totally at the disposal of any earthly power whatever, for everyone has to stand on his own feet responsible before his Creator. So earthly power can only properly be exercised when this freedom of the individual is taken into account, and when this differentiated equality at the crucial point is allowed for. The man in power does not hold or use his power in his own name or for his own purposes. It is forbidden him to exceed the bounds set by the inalienable freedom of the person as such; if he does so, he sins heavily against the truth. He can only exercise power as one commissioned, entrusted with a special mission in the general scheme of human labour; he may occupy a key position in human affairs but it gives him no ultimate rights over others.

This holds good of every form of power, whatever its nature may be and whatever rank its bearer holds; whether he is termed monarch or president or whatever it may be. It is the only conception of power that does not offend human dignity, for it includes a sense of being answerable to something beyond human considerations. And it confines itself to departments of life that naturally require such division of functions, with authorities and subordinates, and admits that ultimate reality is beyond its scope. It makes no claim to have anything to say as to a final appraisal of those in command and those subject to them, nor as to their eternal destiny. From the religious point of view, that is to say in relation to the whole of reality, power may only be exercised as a charge from God. For it comes from him; all power issues from reality, and all finite reality is of God's creation.

Hence obedience is only honourable in so far as it goes out beyond and through the man giving orders, as a service rendered to a common cause, and in the last resort when it is done for the sake of God's will. Obedience needs this religious base if it is truly and fully to give human dignity its due and safeguard personal freedom. For freely accepted subordination is not submission to a man, whoever he may be, but to God's representative, of whose will this man is the agent, whether he is personally fit for it or not; whether he knows it or not; whether he believes he possesses rights to act as he feels inclined, or knows that he is responsible before God for the exercise of his power.

Of its very nature religious obedience is a particularly good vehicle for turning the relations of men to one another into a corporative effort where each plays his own part, and for allowing each to make his own appropriate contribution to the job as a whole: it implies a corporation of different people each with a different section of work to do, the direction of the work and the making of decisions being but one of those charges, one among many, undertaken in the name of all and in the service of the whole. Forceful measures will be less and less in evidence, confined to those cases where bad will or incorrigible lack of judgement rocks the boat. When materialism declares it can rid the world of power, we have to do with a portentous misconception of the nature of force and power, a misconception that is actually centuries out of date. It is amazing that materialism, of all things, should make such claims, when it refuses to recognize any power except the power of matter and what issues from it, which is sheer blind force. But where the independence and freedom of the spirit are denied, this force is delivered into the hands of boundless egoism, causing untold suffering, degradation and distress. Only the spirit that is itself, independent and self-contained, possesses freedom, and the source of its freedom is the absolute freedom of God, who is his own ground.

Religious obedience is therefore valuable in creating social freedom and bringing about a recognition of men's intrinsic equality, whatever grading may be necessary in regard to everyday affairs. It alone keeps one man from letting power run away with him and another from losing his self-respect and lapsing into confirmed slavery. When Christianity appeared, worldly power lost the glamour of divinity that wrapped about it in heathen times, when nothing more exalted was known, when man submitted to it unreservedly in dread and awe. God is the fullness of power, but not in the way the heathen saw it. The power they knew of was rejected by Christ as ultimately powerless, in favour of that true power his earthly vulnerability made evident: the power of self-surrendering love. It exceeds all other power and subdues it, for it alone has the promise of eternity. Intrinsically and essentially, it never encounters failure. And all who have part in it are happy and blessed.

Thus, as the union of our own will to the will of Christ, obedience leads to perfection in loving God and in remaining serene whatever happens on earth. It brings release from the last degree of estrangement from self—that of seeking merit and esteem for oneself in what one is not: in outward successes, in other people's opinion. In God, as his own very foundation, man finds himself. Obedience admits a man to Christ's own self-surrender to the Father. But Christ's obedience to the Father was simply the inclusion of his human nature and human will in what he is as divine Person (John 1. 1 ff.). His humanity entered the inmost circle of God's life and partook of it. Through Christ's obedience, man is admitted into this act of the Man Christ and is thereby accepted into the divine life to be one with it in love. There is no other way to the Father but the way of participation in the loving obedience of the Son. Only through him does man live as child of God.

And as the movement of mutual love between Father and Son forms the unity whence proceeds the Holy Spirit, who is eternal pure conceiving in Person, obedience so understood arises from the inward-dwelling spirit as from its own source of origin, that all things may be brought back to the Father through the Son.